Publishing Team:
Recipe Development: Jennifer Wood and Denise Sorom
Copy Editors: Holly Ebel and Margaret Smith
Art Director and Graphic Design: Laurie Geisler
Art Illustration: Carol and Gary Goodding

Published and distributed by Landauer Books
A division of Landauer Corporation
12251 Maffitt Road, Cumming, Iowa 50061

For information, write Jenny's Country Kitchen® Inc.
438 South Main Street, Dover, Minnesota 55929
www.jennyscountrykitchen.com

Printed in China   10 9 8 7 6 5 4 3 2 1

Library of Congress Cataloging-in-Publication Data available upon request.

Hardcover edition ISBN 1-890621-59-5
Tradepaper edition ISBN 1-890621-68-4

JENNY'S ♥ COUNTRY® KITCHEN

Recipes for
Making Homemade
A Little Easier!

Written by Jennifer Wood

Illustrated by Carol and Gary Goodding

Dedication

I owe a special thanks to so many people who have contributed to my success and my ability to fulfill a longtime dream of writing this cookbook.

To my mom, who allowed me to cook out of her "Old Faithful" cookbook as a young girl, and who told the Chiropractor that I could sell a refrigerator to an Eskimo. Do you know he bought $400 in gift baskets before I left that day?

To my Dad, who loved me enough to lay his retirement on the line and co-sign all my business loans because he believed in his little girl! I am glad that you got to retire to a position as Shipping Manager at Jenny's Country Kitchen®—and yes, I know you think you are the CEO!

To my husband, Dan, who faithfully sells all my creations to the whole world and who puts up with being known as "Jenny's husband".

To Josh, my true salesman. I can still remember your first lemonade stand where you raked in a whopping $26 and took us all out for dinner! Whether you like it or not, you are a carbon copy of your mother.

To Josiah, my tender hearted young man. You are wise beyond your years. May God bless you and keep you tenderhearted.

To Danialle, my social little girl who's so full of life and energy. You are truly a blessing. May God give me at least one-tenth of your energy so I can keep up with you!

To my sister, Crystal, who inspired me to go to the farmer's market in the first place! Thanks for running away to Dallas with me. It provided me with the needed laughter to go on with "real life".

To my sister, Clover, who gets things done and made my first "Fall Festival" a success. Let's do it for many years to come.

To the crew at Jenny's Country Kitchen®. To Denise, our cook, who brilliantly applied for a job in the shipping department so that she could get her foot in the door. Your resumé gave you away! To Sue, our first office manager. Thanks for getting us organized! To the old crew in Lincoln, NE for all the years of tying bows and sorting cases. Dan and I miss you terribly. To Laurie, for coming "on board" at just the right moment. Without you, this book would not be here. And to Teresa and the many other people that work or have worked at JCK. You are all very important!

And especially to God, who gave me a very creative and tenacious mind. Thank you for giving me another chance to live a pain free life, for blessing me so abundantly and for showing me that love covers a multitude of sins.

Above all, keep fervent in your love for one another, because love covers a multitude of sins.

1 Peter 4:8 (NASB)

The Wife of Noble Character

A wife of noble character who can find? She is worth far more than rubies. Her husband has full confidence in her and lacks nothing of value. She brings him good, not harm, all the days of her life. She selects wool and flax and works with eager hands. She is like the merchant ships, bringing her food from afar. She gets up while it is still dark; she provides food for her family and portions for her servant girls. She considers a field and buys it; out of her earnings she plants a vineyard. She sets about her work vigorously; her arms are strong for her tasks. She sees that her trading is profitable, and her lamp does not go out at night. In her hand she holds the distaff and grasps the spindle with her fingers. She opens her arms to the poor and extends her hands to the needy. When it snows, she has no fear for her household; for all of them are clothed in scarlet. She makes coverings for her bed; she is clothed in fine linen and purple. Her husband is respected at the city gate, where he takes his seat among the elders of the land. She makes linen garments and sells them, and supplies the merchants with sashes. She is clothed with strength and dignity; she can laugh at the days to come. She speaks with wisdom, and faithful instruction is on her tongue. She watches over the affairs of her household and does not eat the bread of idleness. Her children arise and call her blessed; her husband also, and he praises her: "Many women do noble things, but you surpass them all." Charm is deceptive, and beauty is fleeting; but a woman who fears the Lord is to be praised. Give her the reward she has earned, and let her works bring her praise at the city gate.

Proverbs 31: 10-31 (NIV)

Easy
Mornings

Easy Mornings

Red = base recipes used in many recipes
Blue = pantry-stocking mixes

Green = freezer-stocking recipes
Purple = slow-cooked recipes

Introduction

Mornings have always been a challenge for me. My dream of being a wife and mother who would "rise while it is still dark" brings truth to the verse "the spirit is willing but the flesh is weak." In our family my husband Dan is the early riser. He uses the early morning quiet for prayer time and then gets the kids moving. Where am I? Slowly pulling myself out of bed. There are plenty of times however, when I "rise" to the occasion to prepare a special breakfast.

With my pantry stocker mixes you can have waffles or pancakes on the table in minutes. Make-ahead egg dishes as well as overnight batters give you still more breakfast choices. And who doesn't love a smoothie? Our recipes for these nutritious and high energy drinks will satisfy even the pickiest eater. With a little planning ahead, most of these recipes can be put together the night before, then cooked or baked in the morning. Those tantalizing aromas will have your family racing to gather around the table.

Watch and pray, lest you enter into temptation. The spirit indeed is willing, but the flesh is weak.

Matthew 26: 41

Sue's Pig-in-Switzerland
Quiche

Easy Mornings

An old favorite made new by our office manager, Sue. To save time, you can buy ham precooked and cubed in the deli section of most grocery stores.

1 Easy Rolling Pie Crust, page 112
3/4 cup grated Swiss cheese
1 1/2 cups cubed ham
2 eggs
1 cup half and half
1 1/2 teaspoons Dijon mustard
1/8 teaspoon ground black or white pepper

Heat the oven to 350°F. Roll out the dough and line a pie plate. Bake the pie shell for 5 to 7 minutes or until very lightly browned. Cool slightly.

Meanwhile, increase the oven temperature to 375°F. Sprinkle the grated cheese and cubed ham into the baked pie shell.

In a bowl, beat together the eggs, half and half, mustard, and pepper. Pour the egg mixture over the cheese and ham in the pie shell. Bake for 45 minutes or until firm in the center and lightly browned along the outer rim. Serve hot!

Serve with Jenny's English Toffee Creamer... and Jenny's Breakfast Blend Coffee!

Serve with fresh fruit and Applesauce and Raisin Bran Refrigerator Muffins, page 137.

Denise's
Apple-Cheddar Quiche

*A*ssemble the quiche the day or evening before, then the next morning all you have to do is heat the oven and bake it.

> 1 Easy Rolling Pie Crust, page 112
> 3 tablespoons butter
> 3 tart apples, peeled, cored, and diced
> 3 tablespoons Jenny's Mulling Spice, or any mulling spice
> 1 1/2 cups grated cheddar cheese
> 3 whole eggs
> 2 egg yolks
> 1 cup cottage cheese
> 1 1/2 cups half-and-half
> 1 teaspoon sugar
> 1/4 teaspoon cinnamon

Heat the oven to 350°F. Roll out the dough and line a pie plate. Bake the pie shell for 5 to 7 minutes or until very lightly browned. Cool slightly.

In a medium-size skillet, melt the butter, add the apples and mulling spice and sauté for 5 minutes. Place the apple mixture in the pie shell then sprinkle the cheddar cheese on the apples.

In a mixing bowl, beat together the 3 whole eggs, the 2 egg yolks, cottage cheese, and half-and-half with an electric mixer until well mixed. Pour the mixture over the apples and cheese. Combine the sugar and cinnamon and sprinkle on the quiche. Bake the quiche immediately or refrigerate overnight.

To bake, preheat the oven to 375°F. Bake for 30 to 45 minutes or until firm in the center and lightly browned along the outer rim. Serve hot!

Serve with fresh fruit and toasted whole grain bread.

Sunday Morning
Brunch Casserole

*T*his delicious recipe was sent to us by Flavia Franta of Wabasso, Minnesota. It was a hit and it is so convenient to make the evening before and bake in the morning.

1 (6-ounce) box seasoned croutons
2 cups shredded cheddar cheese
2 pounds pork sausage, cooked and drained (we prefer 1 pound mild and 1 pound spicy sausage combined)
5 eggs
3/4 teaspoon dry mustard
2 cups milk
1 (10 3/4-ounce) can cream of mushroom soup
1/2 cup milk

Easy Mornings

Grease a 9x13-inch baking pan. Layer the croutons in the pan, then layer the cheese over the croutons, then the sausage over the cheese.

In a medium bowl, beat together the eggs, dry mustard, and the 2 cups of milk. Pour the mixture over the sausage, cheese, and croutons. Cover and refrigerate overnight.

The next morning, heat the oven to 300°F. While waiting for the oven to warm, brew a pot of Jenny's House Blend Coffee to enjoy while the casserole is cooking.

In a small bowl, combine the soup and the 1/2 cup of milk. Gently pour the mixture over the casserole. Bake uncovered for 1 1/2 hours or until the egg mixture appears set, the cheese is melted, and the top of the casserole is lightly browned.

For an elegant breakfast serve with little cups of fresh fruit salad, pages 94-95.

Crustless
Egg Quiche

*T*his quiche is very easy and quite elegant. The recipe uses hash browns rather than a pie crust so it's a great one to make for unexpected guests. It can also be made ahead and refrigerated overnight.

> 5 eggs, beaten
> 1 (12-ounce) package frozen hash brown potatoes
>   or equivalent freshly grated potatoes
> 1/4 cup chopped green onion
> 1/2 teaspoon salt
> 1/8 teaspoon black pepper
> 1/2 cup cottage cheese
> 1 cup shredded cheddar cheese, divided
> **6** slices bacon, cooked and crumbled*   *See Time-Saving Tip, page 76.

Grease a pie plate and set aside.

In a large bowl, mix together the eggs, potatoes, onion, salt, pepper, cottage cheese, and 3/4 cup of the cheddar cheese. Pour the mixture into the prepared pie plate. Cover the pie plate and refrigerate overnight, if desired.

To bake, heat the oven to 350°F. Bake for 25 minutes or until set. Remove the quiche from the oven and sprinkle it with the crumbled bacon and the remaining 1/4 cup cheddar cheese. Bake for 5 minutes more or until the cheese is melted. Serve hot.

Serve with Jenny's French Vanilla Creamer ... and Jenny's Breakfast Blend Coffee!

Chilean
Egg Casserole

This delicious egg dish has a Mexican flair! It's easy to make using my Country Corn Bread and Muffin Mix, page 141.

> 1 bag Country Corn Bread and Muffin Mix, page 141
> 2 cups cottage cheese
> 1 pound shredded Monterey jack, cheddar cheese, or a combination
> 1/2 cup butter, melted
> 2 (4-ounce) cans diced green chiles
> 10 eggs, beaten
>
> Toppings: Salsa and sour cream

Heat the oven to 350°F. Grease one 9x13-inch baking dish or two 8-inch square baking dishes.

In a large mixing bowl, beat together all the ingredients with an electric mixer.

Pour the mixture into the prepared baking dish. Bake for 45 minutes or until the eggs are set.

Top each portion with salsa and sour cream. Serve with fresh fruit and toasted slices of sour dough bread.

Easy Mornings

Bake Ahead and Freeze Ahead . . . Bake the casserole in two 8-inch square baking dishes and freeze one of them for later. To serve, thaw overnight in the refrigerator, then cut into squares. Microwave individual servings until hot, then top with sour cream, salsa, grated cheese, and a few black olive slices. Add a green salad and make it a lunch!

Night Before
Blender Pancakes

*T*hese delicate pancakes, beautifully dusted with powdered sugar and topped with Easy Berry Syrup, page 30, are something between a pancake and a crepe. Slice a few fresh peaches to lay alongside and you have a beautiful and tasty meal to serve guests.

> 6 eggs
> 1 cup cottage cheese
> 1/2 cup all-purpose flour
> 1/4 teaspoon salt
> 3 tablespoons vegetable oil or olive oil
> 1/4 cup milk
> 1/2 teaspoon vanilla (see Homemade Vanilla, page 104)

In a blender container, combine all of the ingredients and blend thoroughly. Refrigerate the mixture in the blender container overnight.

The next morning, lightly stir mixture. Oil and heat a griddle over medium heat. For each pancake, pour 1/4 cup of the mixture onto the hot griddle. Once bubbles begin to form, flip the pancake and finish cooking on the opposite side.

Fold each pancake in half, place on a pretty plate, dust with powdered sugar, and top with Easy Berry Syrup, page 30.

Whole Wheat
Freezer Pancake Batter

*I*magine having a pancake batter ready to go as soon as you wake up in the morning. This recipe makes a large batch that can be frozen in one container or several small ones. Top with Easy Berry Syrup, page 30.

1 1/2 cups all-purpose flour
3/4 cup whole wheat flour
1/2 cup sugar
4 teaspoons baking powder
1/2 teaspoon salt
4 eggs
1/2 cup vegetable oil
1 3/4 cups milk

Easy Mornings

In a large bowl, stir together the flours, sugar, baking powder, and salt. Set aside.

In a small bowl, beat together the eggs and oil. Add the egg mixture and the milk to the dry ingredients. Mix with a wire whisk until smooth. Pour the mixture into a labeled freezer container and store up to 6 months.

To make the pancakes:

Thaw the pancake batter in the refrigerator the night before. In the morning, oil and heat a large skillet over medium-high heat. Pour the pancake batter onto the hot skillet in 1/4-cup increments. Once the tops begin to bubble, flip the pancakes and continue cooking on the opposite side until lightly browned.

Cook 'em Up & Freeze Ahead. . . Cook any remaining pancake batter and allow them to cool. Place pancakes between layers of waxed paper and freeze in an airtight container. When the kids are in a hurry, they can zap them in the microwave oven and pour on a little syrup for a quick, hot, and nutritious breakfast!

Blueberry
Freezer Pancake Batter

*T*his is one of our favorites to take camping! It thaws nicely in the cooler and is ready to cook in the morning. This recipe can be made with or without blueberries. For another taste sensation add sliced bananas and some chopped walnuts to the batter after it has thawed. Top with In-A-Pinch Maple Syrup, page 30.

>   2 1/4 cups all-purpose flour
>   1/2 cup sugar
>   4 teaspoons baking powder
>   1/2 teaspoon salt
>   4 eggs
>   1/3 cup vegetable oil
>   1 3/4 cups milk
>   1 cup blueberries

In a large bowl, stir together the flour, sugar, baking powder, and salt. Set aside.

In a small bowl, beat together the eggs and oil. Add the egg mixture and the milk to the dry ingredients and mix with a wire whisk until smooth. Gently fold in the blueberries. Pour the mixture into a labeled freezer container. Store in the freezer up to 6 months.

To make the pancakes:

Thaw the pancake batter in the refrigerator the night before. In the morning, oil and heat a large skillet over medium-high heat. Pour the pancake batter onto the hot skillet in 1/4-cup increments. Once the tops begin to bubble, flip the pancakes and continue cooking on the opposite side until lightly browned.

Overnight Caramel
French Toast

This is a great recipe to make when you have overnight guests. While you're up late visiting over a cup of Jenny's Funky Monkey Mocha, just mix this recipe together, put it in the fridge, and it will be ready to bake in the morning! For higher nutritional value, use whole wheat bread in place of the French bread.

> 1 cup packed brown sugar
> 3/4 cup heavy whipping cream
> 1 loaf French bread, sliced
> 4 eggs
> 1 cup milk
> 2 teaspoons vanilla (see Homemade Vanilla, page 104)
> 1/2 teaspoon nutmeg
> 1/2 teaspoon cinnamon

In a small saucepan, stir together the brown sugar and cream. Cook over medium heat about 10 minutes, stirring constantly. Pour the caramel sauce into the bottom of a 9x13-inch baking dish. Layer bread slices over the caramel sauce to completely cover, tearing bread as needed to fit.

In a medium mixing bowl, beat together the eggs, milk, vanilla, and spices with an electric mixer. Pour the egg mixture over the bread. Cover and refrigerate overnight.

In the morning, heat the oven to 350°F. Bake the casserole, uncovered, for 35 to 40 minutes or until a knife inserted near the center comes out clean.

To serve, top with banana slices and serve with glasses of fresh orange juice.

Easy Mornings

Freeze Ahead
French Toast

*F*rench toast can be a morning staple at your home if you make a large batch and freeze any leftovers to heat and eat later. Making it with whole wheat bread is more nutritious and has less fat than most pre-made brands.

> 8 eggs, beaten
> 2 cups milk
> 1 to 2 tablespoons vanilla (see Homemade Vanilla, page 104)
> 3 tablespoons sugar
> 24 slices whole wheat bread
> Cinnamon

In a large mixing bowl, beat together the eggs, milk, vanilla, and sugar with an electric mixer until well mixed.

Oil and heat a griddle over medium-high heat. Dip the bread slices into the egg mixture, then immediately place on the hot griddle. Fry each slice until lightly browned, flip and continue cooking until lightly browned.

Transfer the French toast to serving plates, sprinkle with cinnamon and top with butter and Easy Berry Syrup, page 30.

To freeze leftover French Toast . . . let the slices cool, place between layers of waxed paper, and freeze in an airtight container. When you or the kids are in a hurry, zap slices in the microwave oven, and serve sprinkled with cinnamon and topped with butter and Easy Berry Syrup, page 30.

Buttermilk
Pancake and Waffle Mix

*T*his great pantry stocker makes a big batch of very tasty pancake and waffle mix. Dry buttermilk powder is available in the baking aisle of most grocery stores.

> 2 cups dry buttermilk powder
> 7 cups all-purpose flour
> 1 cup whole wheat flour
> 3/4 cup sugar
> 8 teaspoons baking powder
> 4 teaspoons baking soda
> 2 teaspoons salt

Easy
Mornings

In a large bowl, combine all the ingredients. Label and date a large container or several small containers. Store this mix, tightly sealed, up to 6 months.

To make pancakes using the Buttermilk Pancake and Waffle Mix:

> In a medium bowl combine:
> 1 beaten egg
> 2 tablespoons vegetable oil
> 1 cup water (use more for thinner pancakes)

Use a wire whisk to blend in 1 1/2 cups of the Buttermilk Pancake and Waffle Mix. Let the batter rest for 5 minutes.

Preheat a lightly oiled griddle over medium-high heat. Pour 1/4 cup of batter onto the griddle for each pancake. When the pancakes begin to bubble, flip and continue cooking until lightly browned.

To make waffles using the Buttermilk Pancake and Waffle Mix:

> In a medium bowl combine:
> 3 eggs
> 1/4 cup vegetable oil
> 2 cups water

Use a wire whisk to blend in approximately 1 1/2 cups of the Buttermilk Pancake and Waffle Mix; the batter may be lumpy. Let the batter rest for 5 minutes or longer.

Follow the waffle iron manufacturer's directions to bake the waffles.

Serve the buttermilk pancakes with butter, and Easy Berry Syrup, page 30.

Cinnamon 'n Oat
Pancake Mix

*H*ere's another hearty and wholesome pancake mix to keep on hand in your pantry—and it's special enough to serve your guests!

2 cups quick-cooking oats
1 cup all-purpose flour
1 cup whole wheat flour
1/2 cup nonfat dry milk powder
1 tablespoon cinnamon
2 teaspoons salt
4 teaspoons baking powder
1/4 teaspoon cream of tartar

In a large bowl, mix together all the ingredients. Label and date two self-sealing storage bags. Divide the mixture evenly between the two bags; store in a cool, dry place.

To make pancakes using the Cinnamon 'n Oat Pancake Mix:

In a large bowl mix together:
2 eggs
3 tablespoons vegetable oil
1 cup water (or more for thinner batter)

Add one bag of the Cinnamon 'n Oat Pancake Mix and combine thoroughly.

Preheat a lightly oiled griddle over medium-high heat. For each pancake, pour 1/4 cup batter onto the hot griddle. When the pancakes bubble, use a spatula to flip them and continue cooking until lightly browned.

Serve the pancakes with butter, In-A-Pinch Maple Syrup, page 30, fresh fruit and milk.

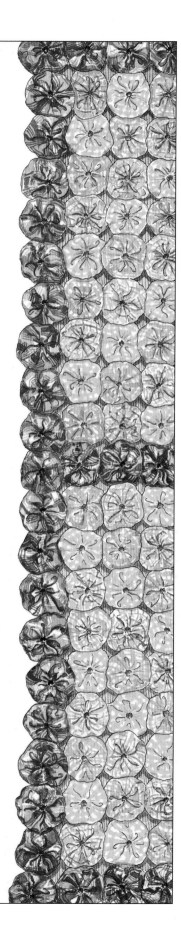

Old Fashioned
Baked Oatmeal Mix

*T*his wholesome breakfast is something between hot granola and cake. Once you try it, I'm sure it will become a favorite at your house! Serve with a simple Blueberry-Banana Fruit Salad, page 95, and glasses of fresh orange juice.

For each bag of mix:

3 cups old fashioned oats
1 cup brown sugar, packed
2 teaspoons baking powder
2 teaspoons ground cinnamon
1 teaspoon salt

*Easy
Mornings*

Combine all the ingredients in a large self-sealing storage bag. Label and date the bag. Store in a cool dry place.

To bake oatmeal using the mix:

1 cup milk
1/3 cup melted butter
2 eggs, beaten
3/4 cup raisins

Preheat the oven to 350°F. Oil an 8-inch square baking dish.

In a large bowl, stir together the milk, melted butter and eggs. Stir the Oatmeal Mix into the liquid ingredients and mix well. Fold in the raisins. Spread the mixture into the prepared baking dish. Bake for 30 to 40 minutes or until set and golden brown.

While piping hot, spoon into bowls and pour milk over each serving.

If you enjoy this . . . make the dry mixture to store in self-sealing bags or tightly sealing containers on your pantry shelf. In the morning, just pull out a bag, mix, bake, and enjoy. For more make-ahead Oatmeal Mixes, see the next page.

Easy
Oatmeal Mixes

*I*t's quick and easy to combine your own oatmeal mixes using your favorite flavors of Jenny's Dessert Coffee Creamers! Here are some of our favorite combinations. The directions are for one serving, so make several bags of your favorite and store them in a large storage container.

Gourmet Cherry Vanilla

1/2 cup quick cooking oatmeal
2 T. Jenny's Cherry Vanilla Creamer
1/4 cup (or more) dried cherries

To serve: In a small bowl, stir together the oatmeal mix and 1/2 cup water. Microwave on high for about 1 minute. Top with fresh milk and enjoy!

Pumpkin Pie

1/2 cup quick cooking oatmeal
2 T. Jenny's Pumpkin Pie Creamer
1/4 cup (or more) raisins

To serve: In a small bowl, stir together the oatmeal mix and 1/2 cup water. Microwave on high for about 1 minute. Top with fresh milk and enjoy!

Cinnamon Apple Crisp

1/2 cup quick cooking oats
2 T. Jenny's Cinnamon Apple
  Crisp Creamer
1/4 cup (or more) dried apples

To serve: In a small bowl, stir together the oatmeal mix and 1/2 cup water. Microwave on high for about 1 minute. Top with fresh milk and enjoy!

White Chocolate & Raspberries

1/2 cup quick cooking oats
2 T. Jenny's Winter White
  Chocolate Creamer
Fresh raspberries

To serve: In a small bowl, stir together the oatmeal mix and 1/2 cup water. Microwave on high for about 1 minute. Top this one with fresh raspberries and milk when done cooking and enjoy!

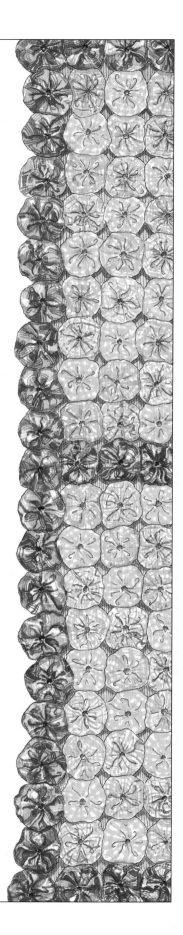

Eye-Opening
Fruit Smoothies

$\mathcal{W}$hen you're really in a pinch for time and you still want to send your kids out the door with good nutrition, fruit smoothies are the answer. We use instant breakfast mixes to whip up our favorites.

Strawberry-Banana
Fruit Smoothie

Easy Mornings

1 cup milk
1 small banana
1 cup frozen strawberries
1 packet vanilla flavored instant breakfast drink mix
1 to 2 tablespoons soy powder (optional)

In a blender container, combine all ingredients and blend thoroughly. Serve immediately.

Very-Berry
Fruit Smoothie

1 cup orange juice
1 packet vanilla flavored instant breakfast drink mix
1 cup frozen berries of your choice
1 to 2 tablespoons soy powder (optional)

In a blender container, combine all ingredients and blend thoroughly. Serve immediately.

Cranberry-Strawberry
Fruit Smoothie

1 cup cranberry juice cocktail
1 packet vanilla flavored instant breakfast drink mix
1 cup frozen strawberries

In a blender container, combine all ingredients and blend thoroughly. Serve immediately.

V-8 Super
Fruit Smoothie

1 cup V-8 Strawberry-Kiwi Drink
1 packet vanilla flavored instant breakfast drink mix
1 ripe banana
1/2 cup frozen triple-berry blend
1/2 cup frozen strawberries

In a blender container, combine all ingredients and blend thoroughly. Serve immediately.

Peanut Butter, Chocolate, and Banana
Fruit Smoothie

1 cup milk
1 packet chocolate flavored instant breakfast drink mix
1 small banana
2 tablespoons creamy peanut butter
4 to 5 ice cubes

In a blender container, combine all ingredients and blend thoroughly. Serve immediately.

Bacon, Egg, and Cheese
Croissants

*C*ooking the bacon the night before cuts your work in half the following morning. You'll be able to whip up these tasty croissants in time for a relaxing breakfast.

For each serving:
1 bakery fresh croissant
1 egg
2 slices bacon, cooked
1 slice American cheese, cut in half

Easy Mornings

Slice the croissant in half lengthwise and set aside on a serving plate. Heat a lightly oiled skillet over medium heat.

In a small bowl, whip the egg with a fork. Pour the egg in the hot skillet. Cook the egg without stirring until the egg begins to set along the bottom and edges. Use a spatula to gently lift the egg, allowing the uncooked portion to flow underneath. Place the cooked bacon alongside the egg to warm. Continue cooking the egg until it is cooked through, looks glossy, and is slightly moist.

Remove the egg and bacon from the skillet and place on a croissant half. Immediately top the egg with the cheese. Place the croissant halves together and heat the sandwich in the microwave oven for 10 seconds or more to slightly melt the cheese.

Serve the bacon, egg, and cheese croissant with fresh fruit and juice.

Grandpa's
Biscuits and Gravy

$\mathcal{M}$y dad and I both love biscuits and gravy. His secret ingredient is the poultry seasoning, which gives it a richer flavor.

> 1 pound sausage (we prefer Jimmy Dean®)
> 1/4 cup all-purpose flour
> 3 cups milk
> 1/2 teaspoon poultry seasoning
> 1 teaspoon salt
> Black pepper
> Freezer-Stocking Baking Powder Biscuits, page 136, baked

In a skillet brown the sausage until no pink remains. Sprinkle the flour over the sausage and mix together well. One cup at a time, slowly add the milk, stirring constantly. Stir in the seasonings. Cook over medium heat until the mixture begins to bubble and is thickened.

Serve the gravy over warm biscuits along with scrambled eggs and fresh orange juice.

Broil and Serve
English Crab Muffins

Make up a batch of these to store in the freezer. You'll enjoy having them for a special brunch dish that you can prepare in a hurry. Or, use them for hors d'oeuvres by broiling them and cutting into sixths.

1/2 cup butter
1 (4-ounce) jar Old English® cheese spread
1 (6-ounce) can crab meat, drained
4 green onions, finely diced
Dash cayenne pepper
5 English muffins
Paprika, for garnish

In a medium mixing bowl, cream together the butter and cheese with an electric mixer. Add the drained crab meat, diced onions, and a dash of cayenne pepper.

Split the English muffins in half. Spread each half with some of the crab mixture. Place on baking sheets to broil immediately or to prepare for freezing.

To broil the muffins, preheat the broiler. Place the baking sheet approximately 4 inches from the heat and broil until the muffins are heated through and lightly browned.

To freeze for later use, place the baking sheet of muffins in the freezer for about one hour. Remove and store in a tightly sealed container in the freezer until ready to use. To serve, place frozen muffins on a baking sheet, allow to thaw slightly, and broil them as instructed above.

Sprinkle the muffins with paprika, and serve with little fresh fruit cups.

Cheese Grits and Sausage
Casserole

*E*very time I go to Atlanta, I absolutely must stop at the Corner Bakery to eat Cheese Grits. This casserole takes grits a step further with sausage, making it a warm, filling breakfast for cold winter mornings.

1 pound pork sausage, (we prefer Jimmy Dean® mild)
3 cups water
1/2 teaspoon salt
1 cup quick cooking grits
1 1/2 cups shredded cheddar cheese, divided
1/4 cup butter
4 eggs, lightly beaten
1/2 cup milk

Heat the oven to 350°F. Grease a 3-quart baking dish; set aside.

In a heavy skillet, brown the sausage, cooking and stirring until crumbly and there is no pink. Drain off the fat.

In a medium size saucepan, bring water and salt to boiling. Gradually stir in the grits. Reduce the heat, cover, and cook for 5 minutes, stirring occasionally.

Remove from heat. To the grits in the saucepan, add 1 cup of the cheese and the butter; stir to blend. Stir in the eggs, milk, and cooked sausage. Spread the mixture in the prepared baking dish. Sprinkle with the remaining 1/2 cup of cheese.

Bake, uncovered, for 1 hour or until golden brown. Remove from the oven and let stand for 15 minutes before serving.

Serve with toasted whole grain bread and fresh-squeezed orange juice.

In-A-Pinch
Maple Syrup

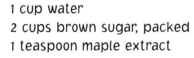

1 cup water
2 cups brown sugar, packed
1 teaspoon maple extract

In a small saucepan, bring the water and brown sugar to boiling, stirring to completely dissolve the sugar.

Remove the mixture from the heat. Stir in the maple extract. Allow the syrup to cool enough to serve.

*Easy
Mornings*

Easy
Berry Syrup

3 cups berries, fresh or frozen, any combination
3 cups sugar
1 cup water
2 tablespoons lemon juice

In a medium size saucepan, mix together the berries, sugar, and water. Simmer, uncovered, over medium heat for 30 minutes, stirring often. Remove from heat and stir in the lemon juice.

Serve the syrup warm over pancakes or waffles. Cool any remaining syrup and store it, sealed, in the refrigerator up to 3 months.

Fresh 'n Simple
Strawberry Jam

1 pound fresh strawberries
1 pound sugar (2 cups)
1 tablespoons lemon juice

Wash and remove the stems from the strawberries. Slice or mash the strawberries. Place in a heavy saucepan, add the sugar and lemon juice, and cook over medium heat. Slowly bring the mixture to a rolling boil; cook for 20 minutes.

Cool the jam in the saucepan. Transfer to glass jars with lids that seal. Store the jam in the refrigerator. Use the jam to top Freezer-Stocking Biscuits, page 136.

Jenny's
Bagel Spread

*I*t's so easy to make flavored cream cheese using Jenny's Dessert Coffee Creamers. Use to top bagels or serve with graham crackers for a quick snack. Here are some of our favorite flavors.

3 ounces cream cheese
2 tablespoons Jenny's Dessert Coffee Creamer (your choice of flavors)

Mix ingredients well and enjoy.

Winter White Chocolate — delicious served with graham cracker sticks.

Cinnamon Apple Crisp — a great bagel topper.

Pumpkin Pie — best served on whole grain bagels.

Gingerbread Cookie — serve with crisp ginger snaps.

Make
Ahead
Main
Dishes

Make Ahead Main Dishes

Red = base recipes used in many recipes
Blue = pantry-stocking mixes

Green = freezer-stocking recipes
Purple = slow-cooked recipes

Introduction

*I*n today's busy world anything that can be made ahead is both a time-saver and a life-saver. Here are my recipes that provide hearty, delicious and satisfying meals that take just minutes to put together. Most can be made ahead and refrigerated, frozen, or simmered in the slow cooker. They include all sorts of family favorites from mouth-watering chicken enchiladas to spaghetti to barbecue beef and meatloaf. Best of all, none of them are difficult nor require any special ingredients. These are real recipes for real families. And just because they are quick and easy does not mean they are not wholesome and nutritious. They are. These recipes are also the perfect answer for a friend in need, or to pull out of the freezer and take to a potluck. Best of all with a single organized trip to the market for a few ingredients you can fix and freeze all sorts of meals for the busy weeks ahead.

Let them do good, that they be rich in good works, ready to give, willing to share.

1 Timothy 6: 18

Easy Shredded
Chicken Breasts

*I*t's easy to make shredded chicken breasts when you use your slow cooker and plan ahead a little. Start the chicken cooking the night before, shred it in the morning, and use it in any of the recipes listed below.

> 8 skinless boneless chicken breasts
> 4 chicken flavored bouillon cubes, or equivalent
> Salt and pepper to taste
> Water to cover

Make Ahead Main Dishes

In a slow cooker, place the chicken breasts, bouillon cubes, salt, pepper, and water filling the pot to not more than three-quarters full. Cook on low setting overnight. The next morning, voilà! When you awake, half of the work is done. Cool and shred the chicken.

Reserve and freeze the chicken broth in 1 cup portions for later use.

Use Easy Shredded Chicken Breasts In These Recipes:

Creamy Chicken Enchiladas, pg. 37
Paprika Chicken with Rice, pg. 38
Chicken and Stuffing Casserole, pg. 39
Cindy's Potluck Chicken Bake, pg. 40
Old Fashioned Chicken Pot Pie, pg. 41
Chicken Tortilla Soup, pg. 42
Creamy Chicken and Wild Rice Soup, pg. 43

Coming up short on chicken? In a pinch, substitute one 13-ounce can of chicken breast for each cup of Easy Shredded Chicken Breast called for in a recipe.

Creamy
Chicken Enchiladas

*T*hese chicken enchiladas are uniquely yummy and easy to make! This recipe can be doubled so you can freeze one pan of enchiladas for later.

    4 cups Easy Shredded Chicken Breasts, facing page
    1 (15-ounce) can cream-style corn
    1 (10 3/4-ounce) can cream of celery or cream of chicken soup*, undiluted
    1 cup (8 ounces) sour cream
    4 cups shredded cheddar cheese, divided
    1 (4-ounce) can chopped green chiles
    1 (16-ounce) can black beans (or any beans), drained
    1 package 10-inch flour tortilla shells

Lightly oil a 9x13-inch baking dish and set aside. Set aside 1 cup of the shredded cheese and the tortilla shells.

In a large bowl, combine all the remaining ingredients; set aside 1/3 of the chicken mixture. Evenly divide the remaining mixture among 7 or 8 tortilla shells. Roll up the tortillas and place them, seam sides down, in the prepared baking dish. Spread the reserved chicken mixture and cheese on top of the tortillas. Bake the casserole now, or cover and tightly wrap it to store in the refrigerator up to two days or in the freezer up to three months.

To bake: Thaw the enchiladas in the refrigerator if frozen. Heat the oven to 350°F. Bake the enchiladas, uncovered, about 1 hour or until heated through.

*Reduced calorie and low-sodium soups work fine.

Serve with a fresh green salad, berries, and a glass of Jenny's Peach Tea.

Paprika

Chicken with Rice

Make Ahead Main Dishes

$\mathcal{T}$his is such a creamy and comforting casserole. It's one of my favorites to take to a potluck or to give to a friend in need because it can be made up ahead and stored in the refrigerator.

> 3 cups cooked instant rice
> 1/4 cup butter
> 1/4 cup finely chopped onion
> 1 teaspoon dried minced garlic
> 2 teaspoons paprika
> 1 teaspoon salt
> 1/2 teaspoon black pepper
> 1 cup Easy Shredded Chicken Breasts, page 36
> 1/2 cup all-purpose flour
> 1 1/4 cups chicken broth
> 1 cup milk

Cook the rice according to package directions; set aside and keep warm. Lightly oil a 2-quart baking dish.

In a large stock pot, melt the butter over medium heat . Add the onion and minced garlic and saute until the onion is tender. Add the paprika, salt, pepper, and cooked chicken; mix well. Sprinkle the flour over the chicken mixture and stir to combine. Gradually pour the chicken broth into the mixture, stirring constantly. Cook until the mixture begins to thicken. Stir in the cooked rice and milk; cook for 5 minutes longer.

Remove the stock pot from the heat and transfer the chicken and rice mixture to the prepared baking dish. Bake the casserole now, or cover it and wrap it tightly to store in the refrigerator up to two days or in the freezer up to three months.

To bake: Thaw the casserole in the refrigerator if frozen. Heat the oven to 350°F. Bake, uncovered, for 30 minutes or until heated through.

Chicken and Stuffing
Casserole

*T*his simple-to-make recipe can be made ahead and refrigerated to heat and serve later. It's also great for using leftover turkey from Thanksgiving.

    1 (6-ounce) package stuffing mix for chicken
    2 cups Easy Shredded Chicken Breasts, page 36, or turkey
    1 (10 3/4-ounce) can cream of chicken or cream or celery soup*, undiluted
    1/3 cup sour cream

Prepare stuffing mix according to package directions; set aside. Lightly oil a 2-quart baking dish; place the chicken in the prepared dish.

In a small bowl, mix together the soup and the sour cream. Combine well. Pour the soup mixture over the chicken in the baking dish. Spoon the stuffing evenly over all. Bake the casserole now or cover it and wrap it tightly to store in the refrigerator up to two days.

To bake the casserole, heat the oven to 375°F. Bake uncovered, for 35 minutes or until bubbly.

*Reduced calorie and low sodium soups work fine.

Serve either casserole with frozen green beans cooked with butter and salt. Add a Strawberry-Banana Fruit Salad, page 95, whole grain bread and butter, and you'll have a complete meal.

39

Cindy's Potluck
Chicken Bake

*C*indy brought this recipe to a potluck at Bible study one day. It was so good I had to get the recipe! It's very rich and creamy with great crunch!

2 cups Easy Shredded Chicken Breasts, page 36
1 to 2 cups diced celery (your choice)
1/2 cup diced onion
1 cup (8 ounces) sour cream
3/4 cup real mayonnaise
1/2 cup sliced almonds
1 cup shredded cheddar cheese
1/2 cup crushed potato chips or Buttered Crumbs, page 77

Heat the oven to 350°F. Lightly grease a 2-quart baking dish; set aside.

In a large bowl, mix together the shredded chicken, celery, onion, sour cream, mayonnaise, and almonds. Place the mixture in the prepared baking dish. Sprinkle with the cheese and potato chips or crumbs.

Bake for 30 minutes or until heated through.

Jenny's Iced English Toffee Twister

1 cup water
1/3 cup Jenny's White Chocolate Latté Mix
2 tablespoons Jenny's English Toffee Creamer
5-6 ice cubes

In a blender container, combine all ingredients and blend thoroughly. Serve immediately.

Serve with a Cranberry and Walnut Salad, page 92 and chilled mugs of Jenny's Iced English Toffee Twister, see recipe above.

Make Ahead Main Dishes

Old Fashioned
Chicken Pot Pie

This hearty chicken pie is simple to make using Easy Shredded Chicken Breasts, page 36, and Easy Rolling Pie Crusts, page 112. Add the ease of packaged diced potatoes and frozen vegetables and you're sure to love this recipe. It makes a very full two-quart casserole so there is likely to be plenty for company or for leftovers.

> 2 Easy Rolling Pie Crusts, page112
> 1 (8-ounce) package frozen peas and carrots
> 1 (1-pound, 4-ounce) package diced potatoes with onions
> 2 cups water
> 1/2 teaspoon salt
> 4 cups Easy Shredded Chicken Breasts, page 36
> 1/4 cup butter
> 6 tablespoons flour
> 3 cups chicken broth (from Easy Shredded Chicken Breasts, if available)
> Salt and pepper
> Seasoning salt
> 1 egg, slightly beaten

Heat the oven to 425° F. Roll out a pie crust to line a 2-quart baking dish, fitting to top edges as well as possible. Roll out a crust to fit the top of the baking dish. Set aside the dish and the top crust.

In a large saucepan, place the frozen peas and carrots, the diced potatoes with onions, the 2 cups of water, and the salt. Bring to boiling over medium heat. Reduce the heat and simmer, covered, for about 5 minutes. Drain off the water. Place the shredded chicken and vegetables in the pastry-lined baking dish.

In a medium size sauce pan, melt the butter over medium heat. Stir in the flour and mix well. Slowly mix in the chicken broth with a wire whip. Cook the mixture until bubbly and thickened. Season to taste with salt and pepper and seasoning salt. Pour the thickened broth over the chicken and vegetables in the baking dish.

Place the top crust on and pinch the crust edges together to seal. Cut slits in the top crust to allow steam to escape during baking. Brush the egg on the crust. Bake for 30 minutes or until top crust is golden brown and the contents are bubbling.

Chicken-Tortilla
Soup

*D*enise made this up while recipe-testing for us, and it's since become a big hit. It's a fuss-free recipe that can be slow-cooked all day, and the leftovers can be frozen in single serve portions for quick lunch fare.

2 tablespoons butter
1/2 teaspoon minced garlic
2 to 3 cups Easy Shredded Chicken Breasts, page 36
2 (14 1/2-ounce) cans chicken broth
2 (14 1/2-ounce) cans stewed tomatoes or 2 quarts home canned tomatoes
1 cup salsa
1/2 cup chopped fresh cilantro
1 tablespoon ground cumin
1 to 2 chicken bouillon cubes

Toppings: Shredded cheddar cheese, sour cream, tortilla chips

In a slow cooker, saute the butter and garlic on high setting. Turn the setting to low. Add the chicken, broth, tomatoes, salsa, cilantro, cumin, and bouillon cubes to the cooker. Cook on low setting for 8 to 10 hours.

Ladle the soup into bowls and top with shredded cheese, sour cream, and crushed tortilla chips.

Serve with some Country Corn Bread, page 141 and mugs of Jenny's refreshing Raspberry Lemonade.

Creamy Chicken and Wild Rice
Soup

*P*erfect to serve on a cold winter's day! This would be a good way to use up your frozen chicken broth from making Easy Shredded Chicken Breasts. If you don't have enough, just use canned or instant broth.

9 cups chicken broth
1 cup uncooked wild rice
1 medium onion, diced
1 cup shredded carrot
3 cups milk
6 tablespoons all-purpose flour
1/2 teaspoon black pepper
1 1/2 cups Easy Shredded Chicken Breasts, page 36

Toppings: Shredded cheddar cheese, chives

In a large saucepan, combine the chicken broth and the wild rice. Bring to boiling, reduce heat, cover, and simmer for 50 minutes or until rice is soft. Stir in the diced onions and shredded carrots; simmer for 5 to 10 minutes longer or until tender.

In a small bowl, whisk together the milk, flour, and pepper. Stir the milk mixture into the rice mixture, and cook until thickened and bubbly, stirring frequently. Add chicken and heat through but do not boil.

Ladle the soup into bowls and top with shredded cheese and chives.

Serve with some Fresh Berry Muffins, page 140, a simple salad and mugs of Jenny's Raspberry Iced Tea.

Quick and Handy
Hamburger

*F*rying ground beef in bulk saves time and money! When you get it home from the grocery store, cook the hamburger, divide into approximately 1-pound portions, and freeze to use in any of the following recipes. Just try it once, and you'll love the convenience of having this cooked and on hand!

8 to 10 pounds fresh ground beef
3 to 4 large onions, finely diced
Salt and pepper to taste
1-quart freezer bags

Make Ahead Main Dishes

In a large skillet, cook the ground beef and onions over medium heat, breaking up the meat to prevent large chunks. Add salt and pepper to taste and cool.

Label and date the freezer bags. Place 2 to 2 1/2 cups in each bag, seal the bags, and place them in the freezer.

Important Note: If you choose to freeze an unbaked casserole, cook 1 pound of fresh ground beef with a finely chopped onion rather than using the frozen, cooked ground beef.

Use Quick and Handy Hamburger In These Recipes:

Easy Tamale Pie, pg. 45
Upside Down Pizza Bake, pg. 46
Baked Enchilada Casserole, pg. 47
Tater-Topped Casserole, pg. 48
Grandma Catherine's
   Slow-Cooked Spaghetti, pg. 49
Mushroom and Swiss Cheese
   One Dish Meal, pg. 50
Grandma's Slow-Simmering Chili, pg. 51

Easy
Tamale Pie

$\mathcal{T}$his quick and easy recipe makes enough for one 9x13 casserole or two 8-inch square casseroles—so you can bake one now and freeze one for later (see important note, facing page).

Cornmeal Topping:
1 egg, well beaten
1 cup milk
1/4 cup melted butter
1 bag Country Corn Bread and Muffin Mix, page 141

Filling:
1 package Quick and Handy Hamburger, facing page, thawed
1 teaspoon ground cumin
1 to 2 tablespoons chili powder
1 (10-ounce) bag frozen corn
1 (4-ounce) can chopped green chiles
1 (4 1/2-ounce) can sliced black olives (or 2.25 ounces drained weight)
1 (16-ounce) can refried beans
1 (15-ounce) can diced tomatoes
2 cups shredded co-jack or cheddar cheese

Toppings: Sour cream, salsa, chopped green onions.

Lightly oil a 9x13-inch baking dish or two 8-inch-square baking dishes; set aside.

In a medium bowl, combine the egg, milk, and melted butter and mix well. Stir in the muffin mix, stirring just until dry ingredients are moistened; set aside.

In a large bowl, combine the filling ingredients; stir until well mixed. Spread the filling in the prepared baking dish.

Spread the muffin batter over the filling. Bake the casserole now, or wrap it to store in the refrigerator up to two days or in the freezer up to three months.

To Bake: Thaw the casserole in the refrigerator if frozen. Heat the oven to 400°F. Bake for 35 to 45 minutes, uncovered, or until the bread is set and golden brown. Add toppings to individual servings.

Upside Down
Pizza Bake

*T*his easy-to-make pizza casserole is one that all kids seem to love! For extra nutrition, substitute 1/2 cup whole wheat flour for 1/2 cup of the all-purpose flour.

1 package Quick and Easy Hamburger, page 44, thawed
1 (15-ounce) jar spaghetti sauce (we prefer Prego® flavored with meat)
Pizza toppings such as sliced mushrooms, diced onion, chopped
   green pepper, cubed cream cheese, or diced tomatoes
1 (8-ounce) package shredded cheddar cheese
1 (8-ounce) package shredded mozzarella cheese

Crust:
1 cup all-purpose flour
2 eggs
1 tablespoon olive oil or vegetable oil
1 cup milk

Grated Parmesan cheese for topping

Make Ahead Main Dishes

Heat the oven to 350°F. In a 9x13-inch baking dish, mix together the thawed hamburger and the spaghetti sauce. Sprinkle with your choice of pizza toppings. Then add the shredded cheeses on top.

In a medium bowl, thoroughly combine the flour, eggs, oil, and milk. Pour over the cheese in the baking dish, distributing as evenly as possible. Bake for 40 minutes or until the top is lightly browned. Let cool about 10 minutes before slicing to serve. To serve, invert the slices onto a plate and sprinkle with Parmesan cheese.

Serve with a tossed green salad, slices of fresh fruit, and milk.

Baked
Enchilada Casserole

$\mathcal{T}$his recipe is easier to make than other enchilada dishes, and I always receive compliments when I make it! It's a large casserole so sometimes I divide it into two 8x8 baking dishes and freeze half to bake at a later date (see important note, page 44).

    1 package Quick and Handy Hamburger, page 44, thawed
    1 (10 3/4-ounce) can cream of mushroom soup*
    1 (10 3/4-ounce) can cream of chicken soup*
    1/2 soup can of milk
    1/2 cup salsa
    1 (4-ounce) can chopped green chiles
    1 (15-ounce) can black beans, drained
    4 cups shredded cheddar cheese, divided
    1 package 7-inch flour tortilla shells

    Toppings: Sour cream, chopped fresh tomatoes, sliced black olives,
        and shredded cheddar cheese

Lightly oil a 9x13-inch baking dish or two 8-inch-square baking dishes; set aside.

In a large bowl, thoroughly mix together the thawed hamburger, soups, milk, salsa, chiles, and beans. Reserve 1 cup of the shredded cheese to top the casserole during baking. Layer some of the meat mixture in the baking pan. Place a layer of tortillas on the meat, tearing tortillas to fit. Layer additional meat, cheese, and tortillas, ending with the meat. Bake the casserole now, or wrap it to store in the refrigerator up to two days or in the freezer up to three months.

To bake: Thaw the casserole in the refrigerator if frozen. Heat the oven to 350°F. Bake, uncovered, for 1 hour or until bubbly. Top with the reserved cheese; bake for 15 minutes more. Remove from the oven and let stand to cool about 10 minutes before serving. Top each slice with sour cream, tomatoes, olives, and cheese for a pretty presentation.

*Reduced calorie and low-sodium soups work fine.

Tater-Topped
Casserole

*T*his traditional casserole is still a favorite at our house. You can vary it by adding different canned vegetables. Shredded cheese gives it a calcium boost too. For a saucier casserole, add an extra can of cream soup, but no additional milk.

*Make
Ahead
Main
Dishes*

1 package Quick and Handy Hamburger, page 44, thawed
1 (10 3/4-ounce) can cream of mushroom, cream of celery,
   or cream of chicken soup*
1/2 soup can of milk
1 (15-ounce) can whole kernel corn, drained
1 (15-ounce) can cut green beans, drained
1 cup shredded cheddar cheese, optional
1 package frozen potato nuggets

Heat the oven to 350°F. In a 9x13-inch baking dish, combine the hamburger, soup, milk, corn, and green beans. Sprinkle with cheese, if desired. Top with the potatoes.

Bake for 1 hour or until the potatoes are browned and the casserole is hot and bubbly.

*Reduced calorie and low-sodium soups work fine.

Jenny's White Raspberry Frappé

1 cup water
2/3 cup Jenny's White Chocolate
   Latté Mix
1/2 cup raspberries
6-7 ice cubes

In a blender container, combine all ingredients and blend thoroughly. Serve immediately.

Serve with whole grain bread, a Strawberry-Banana Fruit Salad, page 95, and chilled mugs of Jenny's White Raspberry Frappé, see recipe above.

Grandma Catherine's
Slow-Cooked Spaghetti

When you stock your pantry with Spaghetti Sauce Mix, and stock your freezer with Quick and Handy Hamburger, page 44, you can whip up spaghetti in a jiff! And guess what? It can be cooked in your slow cooker to boot! How much simpler can you get?

1 package Quick and Handy Hamburger, page 44, thawed
1 bag Spaghetti Sauce Seasoning Mix, see below
1 (6-ounce) can tomato paste
3 cups water
4 ounces dry spaghetti, broken into 4- to 5-inch pieces

Place the hamburger, Spaghetti Sauce Seasoning Mix, tomato paste, and water in a slow cooker. Stir the mixture together. Cook on low setting for 6 to 8 hours, or on high setting for 3 to 5 hours. One hour before serving, adjust to high if cooking on low. Stir in the dry spaghetti and cook for one hour on high setting or until the spaghetti is tender.

Spaghetti Sauce Seasoning Mix

1 tablespoon dried minced onion
1 tablespoon dried parsley flakes
1 tablespoon cornstarch
2 tablespoons dried green pepper
1 1/2 teaspoons salt
1 teaspoon dried minced garlic
1 teaspoon sugar
1 teaspoon Italian seasoning mix

Combine all ingredients in a self-sealing storage bag and store for up to 6 months.

Serve the spaghetti piping hot with a Quick Caesar Salad, page 92. Add some Easy Garlic Cheese Bread, page 58, for a complete meal!

Mushroom and Swiss Cheese
One Dish Meal

*T*his creamy potato and meat dish is a snap to prepare. Swiss cheese and mushrooms give it satisfying taste too!

6 medium potatoes, scrubbed (peeling is optional)
1 package Quick and Handy Hamburger, page 44, thawed
2 (10 3/4-ounce) cans cream of mushroom soup*
1 soup can of milk
1 (8-ounce) package shredded Swiss cheese
2 (4-ounce) cans mushrooms, drained
1/2 teaspoon salt
1/4 teaspoon black pepper

Heat the oven to 375°F. Lightly oil a 9x13-inch baking dish; set aside.

*Reduced calorie and low-sodium soups work fine.

Very thinly slice the potatoes. Layer half of the potatoes in the prepared baking dish.

In a large bowl, mix together the hamburger, soup, milk, cheese, mushrooms, salt, and pepper. Spoon half of the meat mixture over the potatoes; repeat the layers.

Bake for 1 1/2 hours or until the potatoes are fork tender.

Serve piping hot with Joel's Cheddar Biscuits, page 135, fresh corn on the cob and mugs of Jenny's Cherry Limeade.

Grandma's
Slow-Simmering Chili

When the brisk fall weather sets in, you'll definitely want to be at grandma's for her chili. If you can't make it, start this recipe in the morning, and you'll come home to a hot and hearty meal that is a close second!

2 packages Quick and Handy Hamburger, page 44, thawed
3 cups chopped celery
1 (46-ounce) can tomato juice or vegetable juice cocktail
2 (15-ounce) cans kidney or chili beans, drained and rinsed
1/4 cup brown sugar
1/2 cup ketchup
1 to 2 tablespoons chili powder, or to taste
Salt and pepper to taste

Toppings: Corn Chips, shredded cheddar cheese, diced onion

Place all the ingredients in a slow cooker, stirring to combine. Cook on low setting for 6 to 8 hours or on high setting for 3 to 4 hours.

Grandpa says . . . "Substitute BBQ sauce for the ketchup for some extra zip!"

To serve, ladle piping hot chili into bowls. Add your favorite chili toppings such as broken corn chips, shredded cheese and diced onion.

Serve with hot Country Corn Bread, page 141, and cold glasses of milk.

Creamy
Slow-Cooked Pork Chops

*T*his slow-cooked pork chop recipe is perfect for a busy day. It makes it's own gravy and tastes great with mashed potatoes, page 80.

6 pork loin chops
3/4 cup all-purpose flour
1 teaspoon seasoning salt
3 tablespoons cooking oil
1 (10 3/4-ounce) can cream of mushroom soup*
1/3 cup water

*Make
Ahead
Main
Dishes*

Rinse and dry the pork chops. In a small container with a lid or a 1-gallon self-sealing storage bag, mix together the flour and seasoning salt.

In a large frying pan, heat the oil over medium heat. Shake each pork chop in the flour mixture and place in the frying pan. Brown the pork chops on both sides and place them into a slow cooker.

In a medium bowl, mix together the soup and the water until smooth. Pour over the pork chops. Cover and cook on low setting for 6 to 8 hours.

*Reduced calorie and low-sodium soups work fine.

Serve the pork chops, covered in their own gravy, along with mashed potatoes, page 80, fresh corn on the cob and a tossed green salad.

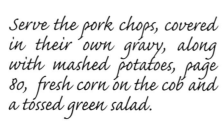

52

Shredded
BBQ Beef Brisket

*T*his recipe is so easy! Put everything in the slow cooker the night before to marinate and refrigerate. You'll be ready to start cooking in the morning!

    4 to 5 pounds beef brisket
    1/8 teaspoon celery salt
    1/4 teaspoon garlic salt
    1/4 teaspoon onion salt
    1/4 teaspoon salt
    3 tablespoons liquid smoke
    2 to 2 1/2 cups bottled barbecue sauce

Place the brisket in a slow cooker. Sprinkle it with celery salt, garlic salt, onion salt, and salt. Pour the liquid smoke on the salted brisket. Cover the cooker and refrigerate the brisket overnight.

In the morning, turn the slow cooker to low setting and cook the brisket for 8 to 10 hours, or until tender. Approximately one hour before cooking is finished, pour barbecue sauce over the meat. Shred the meat with two forks. Spoon the meat mixture onto whole wheat buns.

It's simple to plan a picnic . . . when you have two slow cookers. Simply make the Perked Up BBQ Beans, page 79, in a second slow cooker, then invite your friends over. Plan to make Good Ole Country Coleslaw, page 84, the day before and be sure to have plenty of Jenny's Raspberry Lemonade on hand.

Roast Beef
Dinner & Gravy

*T*his Roast Beef Dinner can be made in an oven or slow cooker, depending on your time schedule for the day.

3 to 4 pounds beef roast (such as boneless chuck roast)
Celery salt
Seasoning salt
Salt and pepper
1 medium onion, sliced
4-6 potatoes, peeled and quartered
1 pound baby carrots

Make Ahead Main Dishes

Heat the oven to 350°F. Rinse the roast under cool running water. Place the meat in a roaster pan and add about 1/2 inch of water to the pan. Sprinkle with celery salt, seasoning salt, and salt and pepper to taste. Place the onion slices on top of the roast and a few in the water. Roast the meat about 1 1/2 hours.

Remove the pan from the oven. Place the potatoes and carrots around the meat. Return the pan to the oven; continue roasting for 45 minutes more or until the potatoes and carrots are tender.

Roast Gravy

1 or 2 beef bouillon cubes
Water
3 tablespoons cornstarch
Salt and pepper

Carefully transfer the broth in the roasting pan to a saucepan. Add bouillon cube(s) and enough water (if needed) to bring the liquid to about 2 cups.

In a bowl, stir together the cornstarch and 1 cup of water. Gradually stir the mixture into the broth, and bring to boiling over medium-high heat, stirring constantly. Season with salt and pepper to taste.

To make this recipe in a slow cooker . . . place everything except the gravy fixings in a slow cooker and cover. Cook on high setting for 1 hour; turn to low setting and continue cooking for 4 or more hours. Remove the potatoes and carrots from the cooker; cover and keep warm. Pour the gravy makings into the cooker, turn to high setting, and cook until the gravy thickens.

Dan's "Cattle Drive"
Beef & Potatoes

I must say that Dan is a John Wayne Fan. We have endured watching most of his movies—at least 100 times each—usually in bits and pieces. One time while getting after the boys, he told them that they should be tougher. After all, John Wayne went on his first cattle drive when he was only 14! The boys' eyes got big as they looked at dad in disbelief and had to remind him that John Wayne wasn't really a cowboy—but just a movie character. This created quite the belly laughs. Anyway, whenever there is leftover steak or roast at our house, everybody loves it when Dad cooks "Cattle Drive" Beef and potatoes!

Leftover roast beef and potatoes, or leftover steak and baked potatoes
Butter
Seasoning salt

Thinly slice the meat and potatoes in approximately 1/4 inch slices. In a large skillet or on a griddle, melt enough butter over medium heat to evenly coat the pan. Lay the meat and potatoes in a single layer in the hot butter. Sprinkle with seasoning salt. Fry the meat and potatoes on both sides until crisp. Serve with ketchup, if desired!

Finish off any of these beef dinners with Rhubarb Custard Pie, page 115 and Jenny's Cafe Blend Coffee.

Hot Roast Beef Sandwiches . . . is another way to use leftover roast beef and gravy. These sandwiches are hearty and filling. Slice and serve the roasted meat on whole wheat bread with sides of mashed potatoes, page 80. Ladle gravy over the sandwiches and potatoes.

Jenny's Famous
Beef 'n Noodles

*T*his slow-cooked meal is the perfect thing to eat on a chilly winter's night—along with a piece of pumpkin pie!

> 2 1/2 to 3 pounds boneless chuck roast
> 6 cups water
> 4 beef bouillon cubes
> 1 teaspoon seasoning salt
> Salt and pepper
> Celery salt
> 2 to 3 cups water
> 1 (16-ounce) bag frozen egg noodles, or for more noodles
>   use 2 (12-ounce) bags

Rinse the roast under cool running water. Place the roast in a slow cooker and cover with water. Add the bouillon cubes, seasoning salt, salt and pepper to taste, and a dash or two of celery salt. Cook the roast for 6 to 8 hours on low setting. Or cook for 1 hour on high setting, then turn to low to finish cooking. The longer it cooks, the more tender the meat becomes.

Transfer the roast to a platter. Shred the meat and discard the fat. Pour the broth into a large saucepan, stir in 2 to 3 cups of water, and bring the broth to boiling. Add the egg noodles and cook until tender. Transfer the shredded beef, cooked noodles, and broth to the slow cooker. Season to taste; heat thoroughly. Serve piping hot!

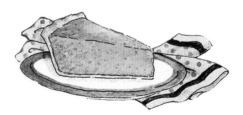

Serve with whole wheat bread, Jenny's Best Pumpkin Pie, page 118, and a big glass of milk.

Make Ahead Main Dishes

Darcy's Slow-Cooked
Honey Ribs

*M*y friend Darcy and I met while living in Portland, Oregon. We have remained friends although we have lived apart for more years than we were neighbors. This recipe makes ribs that are very tender and delicious.

> 2 pounds extra-lean back ribs
>   (also called beef chuck flank-style short ribs)
> 1 (10 1/2-ounce) can beef broth
> 1/2 cup water
> 2 tablespoons maple syrup
> 2 tablespoons honey
> 3 tablespoons soy sauce
> 2 tablespoons barbecue sauce, plus more for topping
> 1/2 teaspoon dry mustard

If the ribs are fatty, place them on a broiler rack and broil for 15 to 20 minutes. Drain off the fat. Cut the ribs in single-serving pieces.

In a slow cooker, combine the remaining ingredients to make a sauce and stir together well. Place the ribs in the sauce. Cover and cook on low setting for 8 to 10 hours (the longer the ribs cook the more tender they become). Remove the cooked ribs from the sauce and place on a serving tray. Top with the remaining sauce; serve hot.

Serve with fresh corn on the cob, Perked Up Baked Beans, page 79 and Good Ole Country Coleslaw, page 84.

Macaroni and Cheese
with Hotdogs

A simple all-American meal that can easily be made in a slow-cooker! This recipe works best when cooked only 3–4 hours at the most. A favorite with kids!

> 1 (16-ounce) package elbow macaroni
> 6 to 8 hot dogs
> 2 (12-ounce) cans low-fat evaporated milk
> 1/2 teaspoon prepared mustard
> 2 (8-ounce) packages shredded processed cheese, such as Velveeta
>   (we prefer 1 American flavor and 1 Cheddar flavor)
> Salt and pepper to taste

Make Ahead Main Dishes

Cook the macaroni, according to the package directions, until just slightly underdone. Drain the macaroni and put it in a lightly oiled slow cooker.

Cut the hotdogs into 1/2-inch chunks. Combine the hotdogs and remaining ingredients with the macaroni and mix well. Cover and cook on low setting for 3 to 4 hours.

Serve with canned fruit cocktail, Easy Garlic Cheese Bread, cookies and milk.

Easy Garlic Cheese Bread . . . Heat the oven to 400°F. Lightly butter about 6 slices of whole wheat or French bread. Sprinkle the buttered bread with garlic salt and a little Parmesan or mozzarella cheese. Toast the slices for about 5 minutes or until lightly browned.

Josh's Cheesy
Chicken Alfredo

*T*his recipe is so simple that even my son Josh has been seen in the kitchen whipping some up!

>1 package Lipton Alfredo Noodles and Sauce
>1 (13-ounce) can chicken breast, drained
>4 slices American cheese

Cook the noodles according to the package directions. Add the chicken and the cheese slices to the noodles, stirring well. Heat through and enjoy.

Crystal's
Mac-In-My-Tummy

*H*ere's an easy way to zip up a box of macaroni and cheese.

>1 box of shells and cheese macaroni
>3 green onions, chopped
>3/4 teaspoon ground turmeric

Prepare macaroni and cheese according to the directions on the box. Add the green onions and turmeric to the cooked mac and cheese, stirring well to evenly distribute the turmeric. Serve hot.

Serve with a simple tossed green salad, fresh fruit and Easy Garlic Cheese Bread, facing page.

Baked Fish With
Creamy White Sauce

*T*his simple way to prepare fish is so delicious, and we all love it here at Jenny's Country Kitchen. The recipe was sent to us by Judy Jacobs of Eau Claire, Wisconsin. She suggests serving it with mashed potatoes, page 80 and steamed asparagus.

> 2 pounds firm fish fillets, such as haddock, perch,
>   or our favorite—orange roughy
> 1/4 cup butter, softened
> 1 cup (8-ounce carton) sour cream
> 1/2 cup grated Parmesan cheese

*Make
Ahead
Main
Dishes*

Heat the oven to 350°F. Lightly grease a baking dish; set aside.

Rinse the fillets under cool running water and pat dry with paper towels. Lay the fish in the baking dish, turning under thin edges to prevent overbrowning or curling as they bake.

In a bowl, mix together the softened butter, sour cream, and Parmesan cheese. Spoon the mixture over the fillets. Bake the fish for 25 to 30 minutes or until the fish flakes easily with a fork.

This fish is also great served with Baked Barley with Mushrooms, page 75, a tossed green salad and Jenny's Raspberry Tea.

Clover's Simple
Crab Fettuccini

$\mathcal{M}$y sister, Clover, 14 months older than I am, is the get-it-done person in the family. This delicious recipe reflects that attitude!

6 ounces fettuccini noodles
1/4 cup butter
1 teaspoon bottled minced garlic
1 (12-ounce) can evaporated 2% milk
1/2 cup grated Parmesan cheese
8 ounces crab or imitation crab
1/8 teaspoon black pepper

Cook the noodles according to the package directions. Meanwhile, in a saucepan, sauté the butter and garlic over medium heat. Carefully pour in the milk; heat until bubbly. Add the Parmesan cheese and stir well. Fold in the crab; sprinkle with pepper. Toss with the hot cooked fettuccini. Serve immediately.

Serve with Strawberry-Spinach Salad, page 93, and fresh bread and butter.

Garlic Time Saver . . . Although you can mince fresh garlic, the bottled version is available in grocery stores—saving you time and trouble. You should know that one fresh garlic clove is equal to 1/2 teaspoon minced garlic. Look for it near the produce aisle, along with ethnic foods or with bottled condiments.

Oven Fried
Chicker

*F*ried chicken is much easier and quicker to make when you have Fried Chicken Coating Mix stocked on your pantry shelf. Add some Slow-Cooked Mashed Potatoes, page 80, and you have an easy home cooked meal!

> 1 fryer chicken, cut up
> 1 1/2 cups Fried Chicken Coating Mix, facing page
> 1/3 cup cooking oil

*Make
Ahead
Main
Dishes*

Heat the oven to 375°F. Rinse the chicken pieces under cool running water and lay them to drain on paper towels.

Place the coating mix in a large bowl with a cover or a 1-gallon self-sealing storage bag. Place chicken pieces, a few at a time, in the coating mix and shake until well coated.

In a large skillet, with an ovenproof handle, heat the oil over medium heat.

Fry the chicken in hot oil for 15 minutes, turning to brown evenly on all sides. Place the skillet in the oven (if the skillet handle is not ovenproof, transfer chicken to an oil coated broiler pan).

Bake the chicken for 45 minutes, until juices run clear when the chicken is tested with a fork. Or use an instant-read thermometer inserted in a meaty portion to test for doneness (170° for breasts, 180° for thighs and drumsticks).

To make gravy with the drippings . . . place the skillet with drippings over medium heat. Stir 1/4 cup all-purpose flour into the drippings, mixing well. When the mixture begins to bubble, slowly add 2 cups of milk or cream, whisking with a wire whisk. Heat until bubbling, whisking constantly. Season to taste with salt and pepper or seasoning salt. Serve over Slow Cooked Mashed Potatoes, page 80, or Freezer-Stocking Baking Powder Biscuits, page 136.

Fried Chicken
Coating Mix

*T*his chicken coating mix is quite zippy! Mix this up and keep it on your pantry shelf for Oven Fried Chicken or use it to coat fresh fish or pork chops. Adjust the seasonings to your taste.

> 4 cups all-purpose flour
> 1 cup corn meal
> 2 tablespoons salt
> 2 tablespoons dry mustard
> 2 tablespoons paprika
> 2 tablespoons garlic salt
> 1 tablespoon celery salt
> 1 tablespoon black pepper
> 1 teaspoon ground ginger

Mix together all ingredients and store in an airtight container. Label and date the container. Use the coating mix to make Oven Fried Chicken, facing page.

Serve with Slow-Cooked Mashed Potatoes, page 80, fresh steamed asparagus, and whole wheat bread. For dessert, serve Josh's Strawberry Rhubarb Crisp, page 123.

Will you pass a "real" chicken leg, please?

If you're tired of the scrawny little chicken legs typically found at your grocery store, buy a roasting chicken and cut it up yourself. It's a much bulkier chicken and it's what my family prefers. You also can buy chickens from local farmers—those taste even better! For complete step-by-step instructions for cutting up a chicken, visit www.fosterfarms.com.

Carol's Fancy
Meat Loaf

Carol brought this microwaveable meat loaf and Seasoned Baked Potato Slices, page 74, when I was recovering from back surgery. The two dishes are great together. I make three loaves at once—one to cook now and two to freeze. They're great to have on hand for a friend in need.

For each loaf:
1 pound fresh ground beef
2/3 cup quick-cooking oats
1/4 cup minced onion
1/4 cup chopped green peppers
1/4 cup chopped celery
1 egg, beaten
1 clove garlic, minced
1 teaspoon dried parsley, or 1 tablespoon fresh minced parsley
1/2 cup tomato juice
3/4 teaspoon salt
1/4 teaspoon black pepper
1/4 cup ketchup, for topping

In a large bowl, combine all of the ingredients except the ketchup, mixing well. Pat the mixture evenly into a 1 1/2-quart baking dish or loaf pan. Bake the meat loaf now, or wrap it to store in the refrigerator for two days or in the freezer up to three months, see tip on facing page.

To cook in a microwave oven: Set to full power for 6 minutes. Pour the ketchup on the loaf. Continue cooking, checking the temperature every 5 minutes until an instant-read thermometer registers 160°F when inserted near center.

To bake the meat loaf in the oven: (which is helpful if you also are baking the Seasoned Baked Potato Slices), Heat the oven to 350°F and bake the meat loaf for 1 hour. Top with ketchup and continue cooking until 160°F

See meat loaf freezing tip, facing page.

Grandma's
Potato Burgers

*T*his recipe, submitted by Carole Schochenmaier of Sauk Rapids, Minnesota, is easy to make ahead and then pop it in the oven for dinner. I've even made it with a bag of freshly shredded hashbrowns and it works just fine.

> 2 pounds fresh ground beef
> 5 or 6 potatoes, peeled and shredded; or 1 (16 ounce) bag
>   of freshly shredded hash browns
> 1 small onion, diced
> 2 (10 3/4-ounce) cans cream of mushroom soup*
> 1/2 cup milk

In a large bowl, mix together the ground beef, potatoes, and onion. Shape the mixture into patties.

In a large skillet, fry the patties over medium heat, until nicely browned on both sides. Transfer the patties to a 3-quart baking dish.

In a small bowl, combine the soup and milk. Pour over the meat patties. Cover and refrigerate until ready to bake.

To bake, heat the oven to 350°F. Bake for 45 to 60 minutes or until the meat is no longer pink in the center or an instant-read thermometer registers 160°F.

*Reduced calorie and low-sodium soups work fine.

Serve with green beans (fresh or frozen) and Joel's Cheddar Biscuits, page 135.

When freezing a meat loaf . . . line a pan with aluminum foil. Place the meat loaf on the foil, then wrap the ends around the meat loaf. Freeze the loaf for an hour or more, remove the foil and frozen meat from the pan, and wrap it in a second layer of foil or put it into a self-sealing freezer bag. This allows you to use the pans for other things.

Freezer-Stocking
Lasagna

$\mathcal{T}$his is by far one of my family's favorite recipes. It makes two to four casseroles—one for the night I make it and the others to freeze, for a hectic day or a friend in need. I use foil pans so when I give away a casserole, there's no need to return the pan.

2 (12-ounce) boxes bowtie pasta
Vegetable or olive oil
2 pounds 90%-lean ground beef
Salt and pepper to taste
2 (24-ounce) jars spaghetti sauce (we prefer Prego® flavored with meat)
1 (15-ounce) can chopped Italian tomatoes
   or 1 additional (15-ounce) jar of spaghetti sauce
2 (24-ounce) cartons small curd cottage cheese
2/3 cup grated Parmesan cheese
8 cups shredded mozzarella cheese (2 pounds), divided
4 eggs, beaten
1/4 cup dried parsley flakes

Cook the pasta according to package directions; do not overcook. Drain the pasta, rinse with cold water, and drain again. Place the pasta in a very large bowl and drizzle approximately 1 tablespoon of vegetable or olive oil over the pasta to prevent it from sticking together. Stir and set aside.

In a skillet, brown the ground beef until no pink remains. Drain off the fat; season the meat with salt and pepper to taste. Mix in the spaghetti sauce and tomatoes; cover and set aside.

To the pasta, add the cottage cheese, Parmesan cheese, 5 cups of mozzarella cheese, the eggs, and parsley flakes, and mix well.

Grease two 9x13-inch baking pans (which will be very full) or four 8-inch square baking pans, or any combination.

Evenly distribute the pasta mixture in the baking pans. Evenly distribute and spread the ground beef mixture on the pasta, spreading to the edges. Wrap the casseroles tightly to store in the refrigerator up to two days or in the freezer up to three months.

Divide the remaining mozzarella cheese into small self-sealing storage bags, according to the number of baking dishes. Label and date the pans and place 1 bag of cheese with each.

To bake: Thaw the casserole in the refrigerator if frozen.

Heat the oven to 350°F. Bake the lasagna, covered, for 45 minutes. Remove the cover, sprinkle on one bag of shredded mozzarella cheese, and bake for 15 minutes more or until heated through. Remove the lasagna from the oven and let set up 10 minutes before cutting it to serve.

Serve with a simple tossed green salad, corn on the cob, Easy Garlic Cheese Bread, page 58, and chilled mugs of Jenny's Peach Tea.

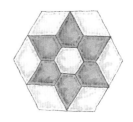

Simple
Sides
and
Salads

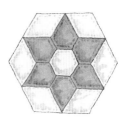

Simple Sides and Salads

Red = base recipes used in many recipes
Blue = pantry-stocking mixes

Green = freezer-stocking recipes
Purple = slow-cooked recipes

Introduction

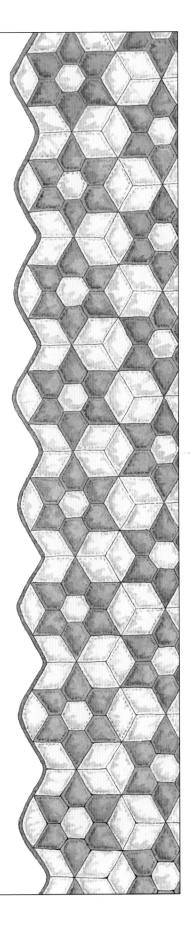

Sides and salads are some of the healthiest dishes we can provide for our families and today they are faster than ever to put together. By adding a few extra ingredients to pre-packaged greens you can have a gourmet salad that everyone will love. Example: Strawberry Spinach Salad, a long-time Wood family favorite. All of my special versions and family favorites are here.

Bring an old fashioned flavor to the table with Mom's Best Potato Salad, Picnic Taco Salad, or Country Market Chicken Salad. Sides and Salads are as important to your menu as the main dish and in fact, sometimes become the main dish.

Easy fruit and sweet salads are a refreshing change from a tossed salad and can also double as a dessert. Try my Cookies and Cream Salad or Strawberry Pretzel Salad the next time you need to take a dish somewhere and get ready for the compliments!

Behold what manner of love the Father has bestowed on us, that we should be called children of God!

1 John 3:1

Picnic
Taco Salad

*T*his salad is filling enough to serve as a main dish, and it's simple to make when you use pre-packaged greens from the grocery store.

3/4 to 1 pound ground beef
1 envelope taco seasoning mix
1/4 cup water
1 (16-ounce) bag prepared iceberg lettuce
1 (10-ounce) bag romaine lettuce
2 ripe tomatoes
3 green onions
1 (15-ounce) can kidney beans, drained and rinsed
2 cups shredded cheddar cheese (8 ounces)
2 cups broken taco-flavored corn chips

Toppings: salad dressing (we prefer ranch), salsa, sour cream

In a skillet, brown the ground beef and drain off the fat. Stir in the taco seasoning mix and the water; simmer, uncovered, until the water evaporates. Set aside to cool.

Meanwhile, rinse and drain the greens. Wash and chop the tomatoes and onions, place them in separate small bowls, cover and refrigerate.

In a large serving bowl, toss together the lettuce, beans, cooled beef mixture, and cheese. Cover and refrigerate until ready to serve.

Just before serving, top the salad with chips, tomatoes, and onions. Serve with salad dressing of your choice, salsa, and sour cream, as desired.

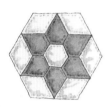

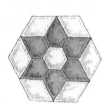

Country Market
Chicken Salad

I first tried a chicken salad like this while visiting in Atlanta. Since then, other chicken salads just don't compare. Try using leftover turkey from Thanksgiving for a slightly different twist.

Dressing:
1 cup real mayonnaise
1 tablespoon Dijon mustard
1 tablespoon packed brown sugar

3 cups cooked, cubed chicken breast (or turkey breast)
1/2 cup raisins
2 green apples, washed, cored, and diced
1/3 cup diced red onion
1 stalk celery, diced
Whole grain raisin bread

Toppings: lettuce, tomatoes

In a large bowl, mix together the mayonnaise, mustard, and brown sugar. Stir in the remaining ingredients and combine well. Cover and refrigerate overnight or for several hours.

To serve, spoon the salad onto slices of whole grain raisin bread. Top with a lettuce leaf, tomato slice, and another bread slice.

Baked Chicken Breasts . . . Heat the oven to 375°F. Lightly oil a 9x13-inch baking dish. Place skinless, boneless chicken breasts in the dish. Bake for 35 to 40 minutes. To test for doneness, juices should run clear and an instant-read thermometer will read 170°F when inserted into a meaty portion of a breast. Cool the chicken breasts and cut into cubes. Freeze any extra cooked and cubed chicken breast to use later in salads and soups.

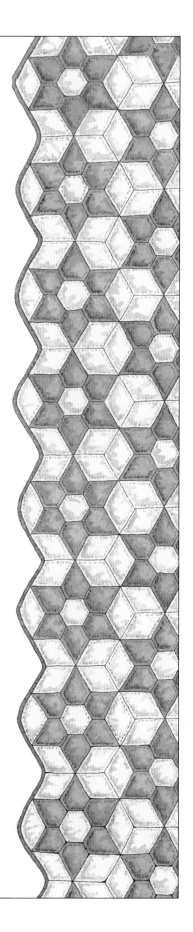

Carol's Seasoned
Potato Slices

*T*his baked potato dish is so simple and goes well with Carol's Fancy Meatloaf, page 64, or any main dish you want to serve. Enjoy.

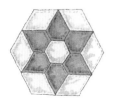

4 large baking potatoes, unpeeled
2 tablespoons butter
2 tablespoons vegetable oil or olive oil
1 teaspoon minced garlic or 2 cloves freshly chopped garlic
1/2 teaspoon salt
1/2 teaspoon dried thyme

*Simple
Sides
and
Salads*

Heat the oven to 400°F. Scrub and slice the unpeeled potatoes in 1/4-inch slices. Layer slices in a 9x13-inch baking dish.

In a small bowl, mix together the butter and oil; drizzle over potato slices. Sprinkle the garlic, salt, and thyme on the potatoes. Bake for 25 to 30 minutes or until the potatoes are fork-tender.

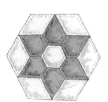

Baked Barley
with Mushrooms

*T*his nutritious recipe goes well with Baked Fish with Creamy White Sauce, page 60. Pine nuts (also called Indian nuts and pignoli) are available at most grocery stores and natural food cooperatives,

1/4 cup butter
1 medium onion, diced
1 cup uncooked pearl barley
1/2 cup pine nuts
2 green onions, thinly sliced
1 (8-ounce) package fresh mushrooms, sliced
1/2 cup fresh parsley, chopped
1/2 teaspoon salt
1/8 teaspoon black pepper
2 (14 1/2-ounce) cans chicken broth (or use reserved frozen broth
   from Easy Shredded Chicken Breasts, page 36)

Heat the oven to 350°F. In a skillet, melt the butter over medium heat. Saute the onion, barley, and pine nuts in hot butter until the barley is lightly browned. Mix in the green onions, mushrooms, and parsley. Season with salt and pepper.

Transfer the mixture to a 2-quart baking dish. Stir in the chicken broth.

Bake for 1 hour and 15 minutes, or until the liquid is absorbed and the barley is tender.

Pine nuts . . . come from several varieties of pine trees grown in China, Italy, Mexico, North Africa, and the Southwestern United States. The labor-intensive process to remove the nut from the pine cone is what makes them expensive—but the taste is worth it! Because pine nuts have a high fat content (hence the flavor) they turn rancid quickly. Store them in airtight containers and refrigerate them up to 3 months or freeze them up to 9 months.

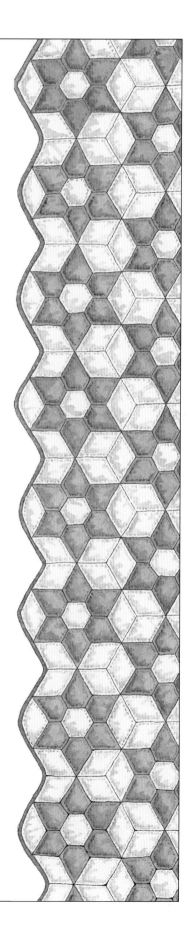

Fresh
Green Beans and Bacon

*T*his is the recipe I make every year as soon as fresh green beans are available at the local farmer's market. It's an old Shaker recipe that I've lightened up a bit.

> 1 pound fresh green beans
> 6 slices bacon*
> 1/4 cup water
> 1/4 teaspoon dried marjoram
> 1/2 teaspoon sugar
> 1/4 cup milk
> Salt and pepper

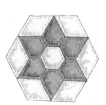

Simple Sides and Salads

Wash and trim the green beans; set them aside.

In a large skillet, cook the bacon over medium heat until crisp. Remove the bacon to a paper towel-lined tray to drain and cool. Reserve 1 tablespoon of bacon drippings in the skillet.

Add the green beans to the reserved bacon drippings. Carefully add the water, marjoram, and sugar. Bring just to boiling. Reduce the heat and simmer, covered, about 10 minutes, stirring occasionally, until the beans are tender yet crisp. Stir in the milk. Season with salt and pepper to taste. Return to simmering and cook for 1 minute more. Crumble and sprinkle the bacon on the beans. Serve the side dish hot.

*Bacon Time Saver . . . When frying bacon, cook a few extra slices. Drain, cool, crumble, and store in a self-sealing freezer bag. Thaw the bacon to top salads (such as JoAnne's Broccoli Salad, page 89), to use on baked potatoes and to spice up gravy.

Creamy
Scalloped Corn

*O*ne of my favorites from my mother's old faithful cookbook—I still remember making it when I was a young girl. I've lowered the salt and fat a bit now that I'm older.

1/4 cup butter
1/2 cup chopped onion
1/4 cup all-purpose flour
1/2 to 1 teaspoon salt
1 teaspoon paprika
1/2 teaspoon dry mustard
Dash black pepper
1 1/2 cups milk
2 (15-ounce) cans whole kernel corn, drained
2 eggs, beaten
Buttered Crumbs

Heat the oven to 350°F. Oil a 2-quart baking dish; set aside.

In a skillet, melt the butter over medium heat. Saute the onion in butter until lightly golden and transparent. Blend in the flour and seasonings. Gradually add the milk, stirring with a wire whisk. Bring to a boil; boil for 1 minute, stirring constantly; remove from heat. Add the corn and eggs, and mix well. Pour the mixture into the prepared baking dish and top with Buttered Crumbs.

Bake for 30 minutes or until set.

Buttered Crumbs

3/4 cup corn flakes
2 tablespoons butter

Place corn flakes in a self-sealing storage bag. Crush the flakes with a rolling pin or the bottom of a cup.

In a saucepan, melt the butter. Pour the crushed flakes into the butter and stir until the cereal is coated. Use the buttered crumbs to top casseroles, such as Creamy Scalloped Corn, above, and Cindy's Potluck Chicken Bake, page 40.

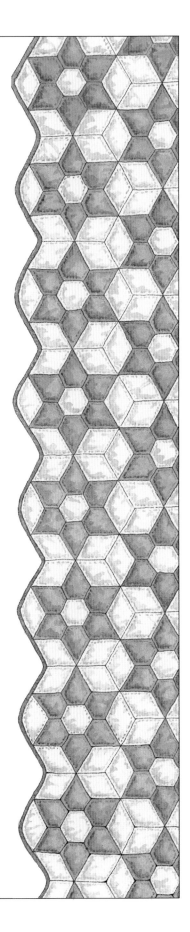

Cheesy
Freezer Mashed Potatoes

*T*hese cheesy mashed potatoes are so yummy that no one will guess they were made ahead and frozen! Double the recipe, bake one tonight, and freeze the remaining in meal-size dishes.

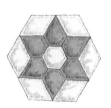

Simple
Sides
and
Salads

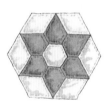

> 10 to 12 medium russet potatoes
> Water
> 2 cups shredded cheddar cheese
> 1 1/2 cups milk
> 1/3 cup butter
> 1 1/2 teaspoons salt
> 2 eggs, beaten

Grease a 9x13-inch baking dish or two 8-inch square baking dishes; set aside.

Peel the potatoes, cut them in fourths, and place them in a large sauce pan or Dutch oven. Cover the potatoes with water; bring to boiling. Reduce the heat and simmer, covered, until the potatoes are tender. Drain the water.

Place the potatoes in a large mixing bowl and add the remaining ingredients. Beat with an electric mixer until well mixed. Spoon the potatoes into the prepared baking dishes. Bake now, or cover them tightly and refrigerate or freeze until ready to use.

To bake the potatoes now or to bake refrigerated potatoes, heat the oven to 350°F. Bake, uncovered, for 1 hour, or until golden brown on top and heated through.

To bake frozen potatoes, heat an oven to 350°F. Bake the frozen potatoes, covered for 1/2 hour, remove the cover and continue baking for 1 hour, or until golden brown on top and heated through.

In A Flash . . . These frozen potatoes also can be heated in the microwave oven. Cook them on medium power for 10-minute intervals, stirring between each interval, until heated through and thickened. This method works well when you grill steaks on a hot summer day because you avoid heating up the kitchen.

Perked Up Baked Beans

*T*his great bean recipe, which can be made in an oven or slow cooker, comes from Angie Johnson of Eyota, Minnesota.

> 2 (1-pound) cans baked beans in tomato sauce
> 1 teaspoon dry mustard
> 3/4 cup packed brown sugar
> 1/2 cup ketchup
> 6 slices bacon, cooked crisp, drained, and crumbled *See Bacon Time
>   Saver Tip, page 76

To bake the beans, heat an oven to 325°F. Lightly oil a 2-quart baking dish.

In a large bowl, mix together the beans, dry mustard, brown sugar, and ketchup. Pour the bean mixture into the prepared dish and sprinkle the top with the cooked, crumbled bacon pieces.

Bake for at least 3 hours.

To cook beans in a slow cooker . . . combine all the ingredients in the cooker. Cook, covered, on low setting for 6 to 8 hours or on high setting for 3 to 4 hours.

Cream Cheese and Corn

> 1 (15-ounce) can whole kernel corn, drained
> 1 (4-ounce) package cream cheese
>   (reduced fat does not work well in this recipe)
> 1 tablespoon butter
> 1/2 teaspoon onion salt
> Salt and pepper to taste

In a small saucepan, combine all the ingredients over medium heat. Heat thoroughly until the cheese is melted. Serve the corn dish hot.

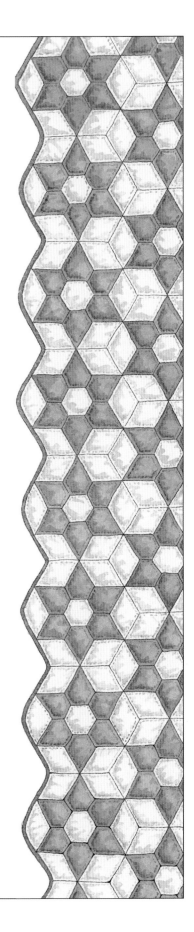

Slow-Cooked
Mashed Potatoes

*A*lthough you can cook these potatoes on a stovetop, they'll never boil over in a slow cooker!

> 12 medium potatoes
> Water
> 1/2 cup milk
> 1 stick butter (1/2 cup), or less if desired
> Salt and pepper

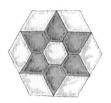

Simple Sides and Salads

Wash, peel, and halve the potatoes. Place them in a slow cooker and cover with water. Cook on high setting for 2 hours or until the potatoes are fork-tender.

Drain the water off the potatoes and place them in a large mixing bowl. Add the milk and butter and whip with an electric mixer. Salt and pepper to taste.

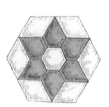

Mashed Potato Variations:

Dilly Mashed Potatoes—Substitute sour cream for half the butter; sprinkle the mashed potatoes with fresh dill.

Garlic-Cheese Mashed Potatoes—Add 1 teaspoon or more crushed garlic and 1 cup of shredded cheddar cheese before mashing the potatoes.

Lisa's
Sweet Potato Casserole

Lisa brought this delicious dish to a ladies' Bible study group. I must have begged her for it about a year—until I finally got the recipe, which uses canned sweet potatoes and is delicious served any time of year!

1 (45-ounce) can sweet potatoes
2 tablespoons butter
1/3 cup packed brown sugar
1 teaspoon vanilla
2 eggs, beaten

Topping:
1/3 cup butter, softened
1/2 cup granulated sugar
1/3 cup all-purpose flour
3/4 cup chopped pecans

Heat the oven to 350°F. Lightly oil a 2-quart baking dish; set aside.

Heat the potatoes* in their own liquid for 10 minutes; drain off liquid. In a large mixing bowl, whip the potatoes, butter, brown sugar, vanilla, and eggs. Place the potato mixture into the prepared baking dish.

In a small bowl, mix together the topping ingredients. Sprinkle the topping on the potatoes. Bake, uncovered, for 30 minutes or until heated through.

*Note: When time is tight, I don't heat the potatoes before whipping them, although the heated potatoes make a creamier casserole.

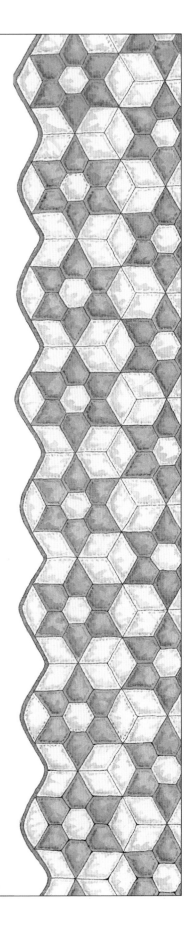

Brown Sugar and Spice
Applesauce

So simple and delicious! Once you eat this, you'll never want to buy applesauce from the store again!

> 8 medium apples, preferably a tart variety
> 2 cups water
> 1 cup brown sugar, packed
> 1/2 teaspoon cinnamon
> 1/4 teaspoon nutmeg
> 1/8 teaspoon allspice
> 1 tablespoon butter

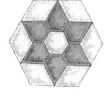

Simple Sides and Salads

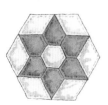

Wash, peel, core, and quarter the apples. Place the apples in a saucepan and cover them with water. Bring to boiling; simmer, covered, about 15 minutes, stirring occasionally, until the apples have the texture you desire. Reduce the heat if necessary to prevent the liquid from completely evaporating. Add the remaining ingredients and heat thoroughly.

Serve warm or cool.

Note: Cooking the apples in water makes for saucier apples. For distinct apple slices, use less water and add the sugar to the water before cooking. Then add the spices and butter when the apple slices are tender.

Apple ABC's . . . Apples provide vitamins A and C and are a good source of fiber. Some good choices for cooking and baking are Baldwin, Cortland, Rome Beauty and Winesap. Check with local orchards to find out which apples are available and do well in your region.

Peanutty
Apple Salad

$\mathcal{T}$ake your childhood favorites of peanut butter and apple slices, add a few more yummies, and you'll have this great salad. Everybody loves it!

2 cups tart apples, washed, cored, and cubed
1 1/2 cups thinly sliced celery
2 cups seedless grapes, washed and cut in half
1 cup miniature marshmallows
1/2 cup peanuts, halved or diced

Dressing:
1/3 cup evaporated milk
1 teaspoon sugar
1/2 teaspoon vanilla (See Homemade Vanilla, page 104)
1/4 cup real mayonnaise
1/4 cup super chunky peanut butter*

In a large bowl, combine the apples, celery, grapes, and the marshmallows.

For the dressing, in a chilled mixing bowl beat the milk until frothy. Add the sugar and vanilla and mix together. Beat in the mayonnaise and the peanut butter. Pour the dressing over the apple mixture and stir to coat. Cover and refrigerate. Just before serving, stir in the halved or diced peanuts.

*Super chunky peanut butter provides lots of texture, but feel free to use whatever you have on hand.

Peanut Butter Nutrition . . . Most commerical peanut butters contain lots of added sugar and hydrogenated fat. Although these keep the peanut butter from separating, they are additions that kids don't need. Look for all-natural peanut butter in the refrigerated section of grocery stores or at local natural food co-ops. You'll appreciate the fresh, truly peanut taste of this niacin and protein rich food.

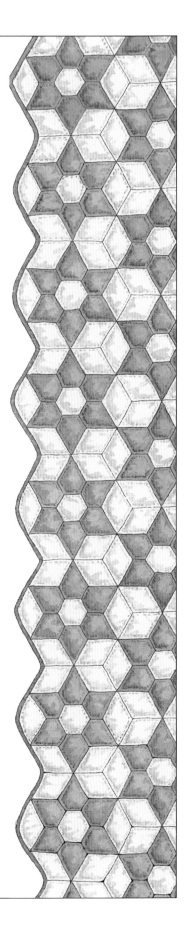

Good Ole
Country Coleslaw

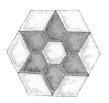

Simple
Sides
and
Salads

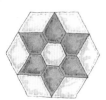

$\mathcal{M}$aking coleslaw has never been easier now that packaged shredded cabbage is sold at grocery stores. Red wine vinegar gives this dressing nice color and distinct taste, however, apple cider vinegar also works just fine.

1 (16-ounce) bag shredded cabbage (4 cups)

Dressing:
1 cup real mayonnaise
2 tablespoons vinegar
4 teaspoons sugar
1 teaspoon celery seed

Put the shredded cabbage in a large bowl; set aside. In a small bowl or a jar with a lid, mix together the dressing ingredients. Pour the dressing over the cabbage and mix well. Cover and refrigerate for several hours before serving.

Good Ole Country Coleslaw is the perfect picnic pleaser! Pair it up with a platter of Oven Fried Chicken, page 62, hard boiled eggs, page 86, and Jenny's Raspberry Lemonade!

Cucumbers in Sour Cream

2 large cucumbers; peeled (if desired) and thinly sliced

Dressing:
3/4 teaspoon salt
1/2 cup sour cream
1 tablespoon lemon juice
1 small onion, sliced into rings
1/4 teaspoon sugar
Dash black pepper

Put the cucumbers in a bowl; set aside. In a small bowl or a jar with a lid, mix together the dressing ingredients. Pour the dressing over the cucumbers and mix well. Cover and refrigerate for several hours before serving.

Crystal's Balsamic Salad

1 (16-ounce) package penne pasta
3/4 cup chopped red onion
2 cucumbers, sliced
1 (15-ounce) can garbanzo beans (chick peas), drained and rinsed
1 1/2 teaspoons Italian seasoning
1 cup balsamic vinegar

Cook the pasta according to package directions. Drain, rinse with cold water, and drain again. Place the pasta in a large plastic bowl with a tightly fitting cover. Add the red onion, cucumbers, beans, seasoning, and vinegar to the pasta. Cover the bowl and shake well to coat the pasta. Marinate in the refrigerator overnight or several hours.

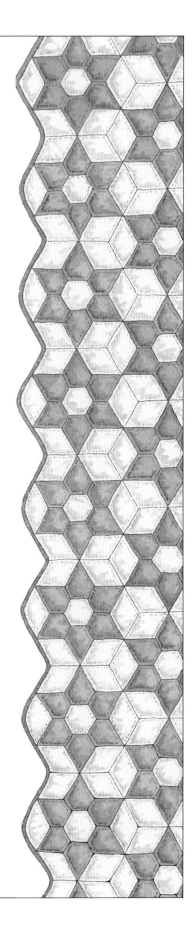

Mom's Best
Potato Salad

*T*his creamy-style potato salad keeps for several days in the refrigerator. There's no vinegar in this recipe, which is the way my family has always made it.

Simple Sides and Salads

6 to 7 cups potatoes, peeled, and cut in 1-inch cubes
Water to cover potatoes
1 1/4 cups real mayonnaise
2 teaspoons Dijon-style mustard
1 teaspoon salt
1/2 teaspoon black pepper
6 hard-cooked eggs, diced or coarsely chopped
2 stalks celery, washed and thinly sliced
1/2 cup diced red onion

In a Dutch Oven or large sauce pan, place potatoes and enough water to cover. Cover and bring to boiling; simmer about 10 minutes or until potatoes are tender yet still hold their shape. Drain, rinse with cold water to cool potatoes, and drain again.

In a large bowl, blend together the mayonnaise, mustard, salt, and pepper. Gently stir in the cooled potatoes, the eggs, celery, and onion. Cover and chill for at least 4 hours to combine the flavors.

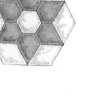

For hard-cooked eggs . . . place eggs in a saucepan; cover eggs with cold water. Heat to boiling, reduce the heat, cover, and simmer gently for 15 minutes. Remove the eggs from the heat, drain, run water over the eggs to cool them, and drain again. Peel right away for the easiest peeling.

Fiesta
Potato Salad

*T*his potato salad has a Mexican flair. It's quite pretty and filling enough to make as a light lunch dish when served with a fresh croissant.

6 to 7 cups potatoes, peeled, and cut in 1-inch cubes
Water to cover potatoes
1 1/2 cups shredded cheddar cheese
1 (16-ounce) can black beans, drained
2/3 cup chopped red sweet pepper
1/2 cup thinly sliced celery
1/3 cup thinly sliced green onions
2 teaspoons minced fresh cilantro or parsley
3/4 cup ranch dressing
1/2 cup chunky-style salsa
1 teaspoon seasoning salt
1/4 teaspoon black pepper

In a Dutch Oven or large sauce pan, place the potatoes and enough water to cover. Cover and bring to boiling; simmer about 10 minutes or until the potatoes are tender yet still hold their shape. Drain, rinse with cold water to cool potatoes, and drain again.

In a large mixing bowl, combine the cheese, beans, sweet pepper, celery, onions, and cilantro or parsley.

In a small bowl, combine the dressing, salsa, seasoning salt, and pepper. Add the potatoes to the bowl with the cheese and bean mixture. Pour the dressing over all and mix well. Cover and refrigerate at least 4 hours to combine the flavors.

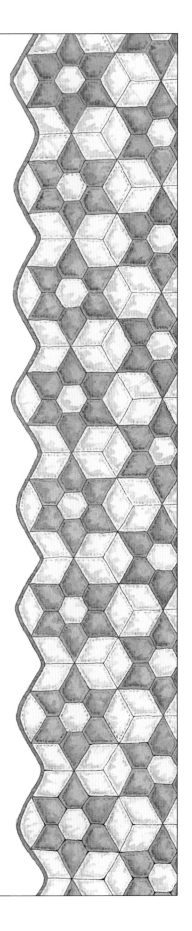

Brandy's
Four Bean Salad

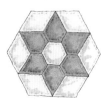

Simple
Sides
and
Salads

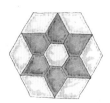

*M*y niece, Brandy, developed this one while testing recipes at Jenny's Country Kitchen. It's very simple to make and it's not as tart as some purchased bean salads. To make it colorful, use red onion.

1 (15-ounce) can green beans, drained
1 (15-ounce) can yellow beans, drained
1 (15-ounce) can kidney beans, drained and rinsed
1 (15-ounce) can garbanzo beans (chick peas), drained and rinsed
1/2 cup chopped green sweet pepper
1 small red onion, chopped or sliced

Dressing:
3/4 cup sugar
2/3 cup vinegar
1/3 cup salad oil
1 teaspoon salt
1 teaspoon black pepper

In a large bowl, mix together the beans, sweet pepper, and onion.

In a small bowl or jar with a lid, mix together the dressing ingredients. Pour the dressing over the bean mixture in the large bowl. Cover and refrigerate for several hours before serving.

JoAnne's
Broccoli Salad

*J*oAnne was my neighbor at the first house Dan and I bought. She was what a neighbor should be: I could borrow an egg from her and we'd chat over the fence. She gave me this recipe when she heard I was writing a cookbook; we tested it and think it's fabulous!

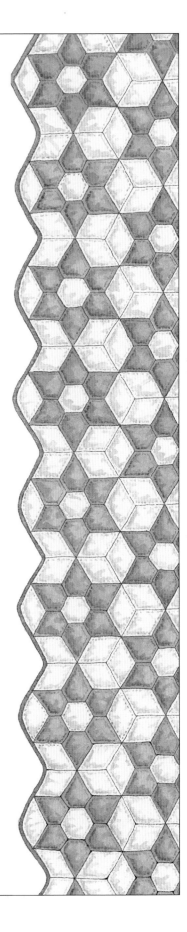

1 large bunch raw broccoli florets
1/2 pound sliced bacon, cooked crisp, drained, and crumbled*
1 cup raisins
1/4 cup chopped green onions
1 cup sunflower seeds

Dressing:
2/3 cup mayonnaise
1/3 cup sugar
1 tablespoon vinegar

In a large bowl, mix together the broccoli florets, bacon, raisins, and onion.

In a small bowl or jar with a lid, mix together the dressing ingredients. Pour the dressing over the broccoli mixture and mix well. Cover and refrigerate for two hours or more. Just before serving, sprinkle the sunflower seeds on the salad.

*See the Bacon Time Saver tip, page 76, for cooking bacon ahead.

Mama Lucia's
Pasta Salad

*W*e've taken a good traditional pasta salad and made it a little easier! This recipe allows for flexibility—feel free to add or subtract ingredients to suit your family's tastes.

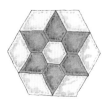

Simple
Sides
and
Salads

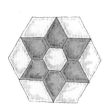

1 (16-ounce) package tri-color pasta
1 cup sliced salami or pepperoni
1 bag ready-to-eat cauliflower florets
1 pint cherry tomatoes, washed and cut in half
1/2 cup grated Parmesan cheese
1 (2.25-ounce) can sliced black olives, drained
1 cup sliced carrots
1/2 small red onion, diced
1 (15-ounce) can garbanzo beans (chick peas), rinsed and drained
1 cup (8 ounces) bottled Italian dressing

Cook the pasta according to the package directions. Drain, rinse, and cool the pasta.

Place the pasta in a large bowl with a tightly fitting cover. Add the remaining ingredients to the pasta and mix well. Cover and refrigerate the salad for several hours. Just before serving, mix the salad again.

Hawaiian
Carrot Salad

*Y*ou can make this refreshing sweet salad the night before you serve it. You'll love it! Some grocery stores sell pre-shredded carrots which makes the salad even simpler!

 4 cups shredded carrots (about 1 lb.)
 1 (15-ounce) can pineapple tidbits, drained (juice reserved)
 1 cup raisins
 3/4 cup flaked coconut
 1 cup real mayonnaise
 3/4 cup cashew halves

In a medium bowl, combine the carrots, pineapple, raisins, and coconut.

In a small bowl, blend together the mayonnaise and 1 tablespoon of the pineapple juice. Pour the mixture over the carrots and stir together to coat the carrots. Cover and refrigerate for 2 hours or more. Before serving, stir in most of the cashews, reserving a few to sprinkle on the salad.

Tossed
Green Salads

$\mathcal{M}$aking fresh green salads is so simple when you use the varieties of packaged greens from grocery stores. Be creative with the mixes, making them sweet or savory, colorful or subdued. Adding a salad with special ingredients really dresses up any meal. Here are a few of my favorite combinations.

Cranberry and Walnut Salad

This salad is colorful, nutritious and delicious. I like to serve it with Joel's Cheddar Biscuits, page 135, too!

> 1 (5-ounce) bag spring mix greens, or gourmet mesclun
> 1 cup dried cranberries
> 1 cup chopped walnuts
> 1 apple, sliced
> Colby cheese
> Salad dressing

Rinse and drain the greens. Divide the greens among serving size bowls. Top the greens in each bowl with some dried cranberries and walnuts. Place a couple of apple slices and a wedge of Colby cheese alongside the greens. Top with your choice of salad dressing.

Quick Caesar Salad

> 1 (10-ounce) bag Italian or Romaine Lettuce
> 1 cup croutons
> 1/2 cup fresh shredded Parmesan cheese
> 1/2 cup classic Caesar dressing

Rinse and drain greens. Toss all the ingredients together in a large bowl. Refrigerate to chill before serving.

Serve chilled with Freezer Lasagna, page 66 or any meal of your choice.

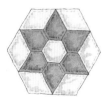

Simple Sides and Salads

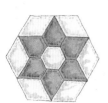

Strawberry-Spinach Salad

This salad goes well with Sue's Pig-in-Switzerland Quiche, page 10, for a beautiful and delicious brunch.

> 1 bag spinach
> 1 pint fresh strawberries, washed and sliced
> Mozzarella cheese, shredded or cubed
> Honey-Poppy Seed Dressing, listed below

Rinse and drain the spinach leaves. Divide the greens among serving-size bowls, top with sliced strawberries and mozzarella cheese. Drizzle dressing over all.

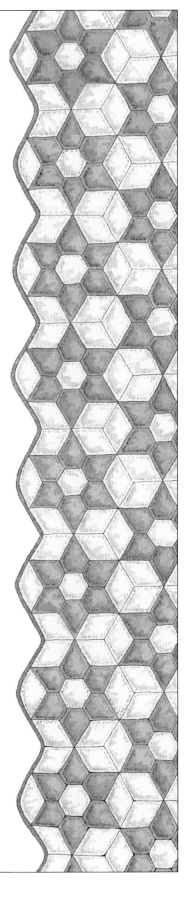

Honey-Poppy Seed Dressing

This light, low calorie dressing is wonderful served over fruit for brunch or on a Strawberry-Spinach Salad, listed above. This recipe makes 1 cup of dressing; you may like it so well that you'll want to double it for large salads.

> 1 (8-ounce) container plain yogurt
> 1 tablespoon poppy seeds
> 1 tablespoon honey (plain or flavored)
> 1 tablespoon orange or lemon juice
> 1/2 teaspoon cider vinegar
> 1/4 teaspoon zest of orange or lemon

In a medium bowl or large jar with a lid, combine all the ingredients. Cover and refrigerate.

Easy
Fruit Salads

*O*ver the years I have discovered that simple fruit salads are a perfect way to perk up meals. The kids love these combinations, so there's never leftovers!

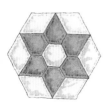

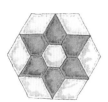

Tropical Fruit Salad

This salad goes fast, so you may want to double it for a crowd of kids. Chilling cans of mandarin orange segments and pineapple chunks for a few hours in the refrigerator makes putting together this chilled salad extra speedy!

> 1 (11-ounce) can mandarin orange segments
> 1 (15-ounce) can pineapple chunks
> 2 bananas

Drain and reserve about half of the juice from both cans of fruit to use in the salad. In a medium bowl, slice the bananas, pour the fruit and juice over the bananas. Gently stir to combine, and serve immediately.

Fresh Berry Fruit Salad

White Chocolate Whipped Topping, page 132, dresses up any variety of fresh berries.

> 1 carton fresh raspberries
> 1 carton fresh blueberries
> 1 pint fresh strawberries
> Mint leaves or sprigs for garnish

Rinse and drain the fresh fruits. Remove the stems from the strawberries and slice them in half.

Fill individual serving dishes with a combination of fresh berries. Top with White Chocolate Whipped Topping, page 132.

Strawberry-Banana Fruit Salad

1 (16-ounce) carton frozen, sweetened, sliced strawberries, thawed
2 or 3 bananas

Place the strawberries in a bowl. Slice the bananas on the strawberries and stir well to combine. Spoon the fruit into dishes and top the fruit with a dollop of Jenny's French Vanilla Whipped Cream, page 132.

Blueberry-Banana Fruit Salad

My kids love to eat frozen blueberries for a sweet treat.

2 or 3 fresh bananas
1 package frozen blueberries, thawed, if desired

Slice the bananas into individual serving dishes. Top each serving with of a few blueberries.

Serve this salad with Old Fashioned Baked Oatmeal, page 22, or anytime.

Apple Slices with Peanut Butter

I serve this to add both protein and fruit to a meal or snack. And what kid doesn't love dipping apple slices into peanut butter?

2 or 3 fresh apples, any variety
Peanut butter

Wash, core, and slice the apples. Place several slices in each serving dish. Scoop peanut butter on the apple slices and serve immediately.

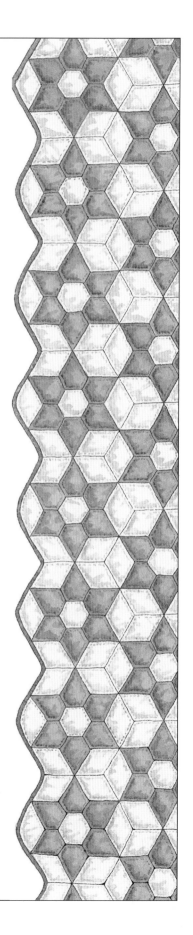

Cookies and Cream
Salad

$\mathcal{K}$ids will just love this salad and It's no wonder, it also makes a great dessert!

1 cup buttermilk
1 (3-ounce) package instant vanilla pudding mix
1 (8-ounce) carton frozen whipped topping, thawed
1 (13-ounce) can pineapple tidbits, drained
2 (11-ounce) cans mandarin orange segments, drained
16 fudge-striped cookies, broken into chunks

Substituting the buttermilk for the milk, prepare the pudding mix according to the package directions, beating with an electric mixer until thick and creamy. Fold in the whipped topping, pineapple, and orange segments. Cover and refrigerate until ready to serve. Just before serving, fold in the broken cookies.

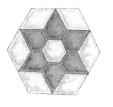

Simple Sides and Salads

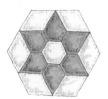

Strawberry
Fruit Fluff Salad

*M*y Aunt Lisa serves this easy-to-make fruit salad at family gatherings, varying the color and flavor according to the holiday. For Christmas—it's strawberry, for Easter—it's orange, and for picnics—it's lime. Make it ahead and refrigerate it until party time.

1 (12-ounce) container cottage cheese
1 (8-ounce) container whipped topping, thawed
1 (3-ounce) box strawberry gelatin
1 cup fresh sliced strawberries, or frozen strawberries, thawed and drained

In a blender container, blend the cottage cheese until smooth*.

In a large bowl, mix together the cottage cheese, whipped topping, and dry gelatin. Stir together until the gelatin dissolves. Reserve a few strawberries for garnish; fold the remaining strawberries in the gelatin mixture. Cover and refrigerate until ready to serve.

*Blending the cottage cheese is optional, my kids prefer not having chunks of cottage cheese.

Other Great Fruit Fluffs:

Lime Fluff: Substitute a box of lime gelatin and use 1 (11-ounce) can of mandarin orange segments (drained), fresh kiwi slices, or 1 (20-ounce) can of pineapple chunks, drained.

Cranberry Raspberry Fluff: Substitute a box of cranberry-raspberry gelatin and fresh or frozen raspberries (thawed and drained). Top with pecans if you like.

Orange Fluff: Substitute a box of orange gelatin and use 1 (11-ounce) can of mandarin oranges, drained.

Clover's
Apple-Cinnamon Gelatin

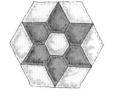

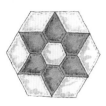

𝓜y kids insist that Aunt Clover bring this salad to every family gathering. They simply love it. For more texture, use chunky homemade applesauce.

2 cups boiling water
1 (6-ounce) package mixed fruit gelatin*
1/2 cup cinnamon red hot candies
2 cups applesauce
Frozen whipped topping, thawed

In a medium bowl, stir the boiling water, gelatin, and candies until the gelatin and candies are melted (10 to 15 minutes). Stir in the applesauce. Pour into a serving dish or gelatin mold. Refrigerate about 2 hours or until firm.

Serve the gelatin from the dish or unmold and invert onto a plate; top individual servings with whipped topping.

*Sugar-free gelatin works just fine.

Jenny's
Strawberry-Pretzel Salad

*T*his is the salad recipe that taught me true humility! We featured it in our second newsletter and failed to list how much cream cheese to add. Needless to say, I had several messages from frustrated cooks. So here it is reprinted and complete. Please try it again—it's well worth the effort!

3/4 cup butter, softened
1/4 cup packed brown sugar
2 1/2 cups crushed pretzels
1 (6-ounce) package strawberry gelatin
2 1/2 cups boiling water
3 cups frozen, sweetened, sliced strawberries, thawed
1 (8-ounce) package cream cheese, softened
1 cup granulated sugar
1 (8-ounce) container frozen whipped topping, thawed

Heat the oven to 350°F. In a mixing bowl, cream together the butter and brown sugar. Mix in the crushed pretzels. Pat the crust mixture into the bottom of a 9x13-inch baking pan. Bake for 10 to 12 minutes. Set aside to cool.

In a medium bowl, dissolve the gelatin in the boiling water. Stir in the strawberries. Chill the gelatin until partially thickened.

In a small mixing bowl, beat together the cream cheese and granulated sugar with an electric mixer until smooth. Fold in the whipped topping. Spread the mixture on the cooled pretzel crust, completely covering the crust. Pour the gelatin and strawberry mixture over the cream cheese layer. Chill until firm.

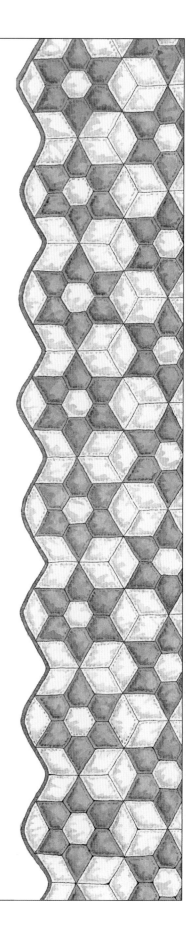

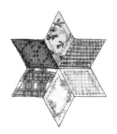

Desserts
and
Breads

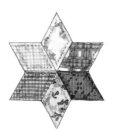

Desserts and Breads

Red = base recipes used in many recipes
Blue = pantry-stocking mixes

Green = freezer-stocking recipes
Purple = slow-cooked recipes

Introduction

*T*he joke at our house is that I like to "eat softly and order a big dessert". We all know there is nothing like a good homemade dessert to end a meal. Here I've given you all sorts of tempting choices sure to satisfy everyone's sweet tooth. I've also included my recipes for cookie balls™, one of the best ways I know of to have an after-school snack ready and waiting for your kids. Your favorite cookie batter is formed into balls, then stored in the freezer ready to pull out and bake.

My versatile Easy Rolling Pie Crust™ and Crisp Topping Mix make for speedy desserts as well. Have you ever had carrot cake baked in a jar? Try my version - it's the best! I've also included make-ahead batters that bring fresh baked goodness to your family in no time at all.

Of course, the perfect accompaniment to all of these is a cup of Jenny's Country Kitchen coffee with creamer; there's plenty of flavors and varieties to fit everyone's tastes.

Let us not become weary in doing good, for at the proper time we will reap a harvest if we do not give up. Therefore, as we have opportunity, let us do good to all people, especially to those who belong to the family of believers.

Galatians 6: 9-10

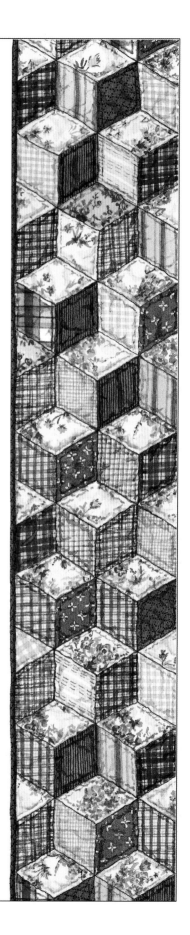

Homemade
Vanilla

*T*he section begins with this recipe for a very good reason. Every good country cook should always have on hand a very large bottle of homemade vanilla! Making it yourself is incredibly easy, it saves you time and money, and you won't be as likely to run out and have to go buy a tiny bottle of imitation vanilla. This is the real stuff!

1 large bottle of inexpensive vodka or bourbon (approximately 1.5 liters)
4 or 5 vanilla beans

Split the vanilla beans lengthwise to expose the small black seeds. Place the vanilla beans in the vodka or bourbon, cap the bottle, and store it in a cool dark place for about a month or until you feel the vanilla aroma is strong enough. This bottle of vanilla should last a long time, and it continues to get better with age. (I wish I could say the same about myself!)

Purchase vanilla beans . . . at gourmet food stores or natural food co-ops. If you can't find them at a reasonable price, please check our website at www.jennyscountrykitchen.com

Desserts and Breads

Making Homemade Cookies
a whole lot easier!

*T*he idea of making cookie balls comes from the fact that, although I am a good cook, I can never finish baking a batch of cookies without burning at least a pan or two. For me, the whole cookie-baking process simply takes too long, and by the time the last pans are baking, I'm busy thinking about and doing other things around the house.

When it became a problem of what kind of cookies to make because each of the kids and my husband all want a different kind, I began freezing balls of cookie dough. Now when we want freshly baked cookies, I simply take out the desired variety and amount from the freezer and bake! Everyone is happy, including myself because I've shaved off hours of preparation time by having these frozen. I am positive that once you try this, you'll never make cookies the old way again.

Tips on Making Cookie Balls™

For nutritional value . . . I use a combination of butter and olive oil. It also helps the cookies turn out chewy on the inside and crispy on the outside. Using whole wheat flour also increases the nutritional value of each cookie. However, you can substitute vegetable oil, shortening, or butter for the total fat, and you can use only all-purpose flour instead of combining it with whole wheat flour. The results will still be delicious.

A necessity for shaping . . . cookie balls is a good cookie scoop. You can usually find them in gourmet kitchen stores—or to order online, check out our website at www.jennyscountrykitchen.com.

Before freezing the entire batch . . . I usually test-bake a few cookies. Use a cookie scoop to shape balls and place them on a cookie sheet. Bake as directed in each recipe. If the cookies spread too far, add more of the whole wheat or all-purpose flour to the cookie dough to achieve the desired texture.

To make cookie balls . . . shape the remaining dough into cookie balls and place them on cookie sheets. Freeze the cookie balls for 1 hour, then transfer the balls to a tightly sealing storage container. The frozen cookie balls stay fresh up to six months.

Oatmeal-Raisin
Cookie Balls™

*T*hese wonderful cookies are filled with whole grains, raisins, and sunflower seeds. These are Dan's absolute favorite and he can even bake them himself!

1 cup butter, softened
1/2 cup light olive oil (or 1/2 cup additional butter)
1 1/2 cups granulated sugar
1 1/2 cups packed brown sugar
3 eggs
2 teaspoons vanilla (see Homemade Vanilla, page 104)
1 1/2 cups all-purpose flour
1 to 1 1/2 cups whole wheat flour
1 1/2 teaspoons salt
1 1/2 teaspoons baking soda
4 1/2 cups old fashioned oats
2 cups raisins
1/4 to 1/2 cup sunflower seeds

In a large mixing bowl, cream together the butter, olive oil, and sugars with an electric mixer until well combined. Beat in the eggs and vanilla and mix well.

In a medium bowl, mix together the 1 1/2 cups all-purpose flour, 1 cup of the whole wheat flour, the salt, and baking soda. Add the dry ingredients to the creamed mixture and blend well. Use a wooden spoon to stir in the oats, raisins, and sunflower seeds.

Freeze the cookie balls according to the directions on page 105.

To bake frozen cookie balls:
Heat the oven to 350°F. Place frozen cookie balls on a cookie sheet, allowing enough room for the cookies to spread while baking. Let stand about 10 minutes to partially thaw. Bake for 12 minutes or until lightly browned.

Desserts and Breads

Chocolate Chip
Cookie Balls™

Warm chocolate chip cookies, right out of the oven, can satisfy my biggest chocoholic, Danialle. I often substitute 1/2 cup whole wheat flour for some of the all-purpose flour to give them a nutritional boost.

> 1 1/2 cups butter, softened
> 1/2 cup light olive oil (or 1/2 cup additional butter)
> 1 1/3 cups granulated sugar
> 1 2/3 cups packed brown sugar
> 4 eggs
> 1 tablespoon vanilla (see Homemade Vanilla, page 104)
> 5 1/2 cups all-purpose flour
> 2 teaspoons salt
> 2 teaspoons baking soda
> 2 (12-ounce) packages milk chocolate or semisweet chocolate chips
> 1 cup chopped walnuts or pecans, (optional)

In a large mixing bowl, cream together the butter, olive oil, and sugars with an electric mixer until well combined. Beat in the eggs and vanilla and mix well.

In a medium bowl, mix together the flour, salt, and baking soda. Add the dry ingredients to the creamed mixture and mix well. If necessary, use a wooden spoon to add the last of the flour. Fold in the chocolate chips and the nuts, if using, until mixed.

Freeze the cookie balls according to the directions on page 105.

To bake frozen cookie balls:
Heat the oven to 350°F. Place frozen cookie balls on a cookie sheet, allowing enough room for the cookies to spread while baking. Let stand about 10 minutes to partially thaw. Bake for 12 minutes or until lightly browned.

Molasses Gingersnap
Cookie Balls™

*M*y son, Joshua, loves the molasses and spices in these cookies! As always, enjoy these cookies served warm from the oven with a cold glass of milk.

3/4 cup butter, softened
1/4 cup light olive oil (or 1/4 cup additional butter)
1 cup packed brown sugar
2/3 cup water
1 1/2 cups unsulphured molasses
6 1/2 cups all-purpose flour
2 teaspoons baking soda
2 teaspoons salt
2 teaspoons ground cinnamon
1 teaspoon ground ginger
1 teaspoon ground cloves
1 teaspoon ground allspice

Desserts and Breads

In a large mixing bowl, cream together the butter, olive oil, and sugar with an electric mixer until well combined. Beat in the water and molasses until well combined.

In a separate large bowl, combine the flour, baking soda, salt, cinnamon, ginger, cloves, and allspice. Gradually blend the dry ingredients into the creamed mixture, using a wooden spoon to stir in the last of the dry ingredients, if necessary. Combine the ingredients well.

Freeze the cookie balls according to the directions on page 105.

To bake frozen cookie balls:
Heat the oven to 350°F. Roll frozen cookie balls in granulated sugar. Place the cookies on a cookie sheet, allowing enough room for the cookies to spread. Let stand for about 10 minutes to partially thaw. Bake for 10 minutes or until lightly browned.

Peanut Butter
Cookie Balls™

*P*eanut butter cookies are my favorite! Grandma Freda uses chunky peanut butter for added texture but any peanut butter works fine. Substituting whole wheat flour for part of the all-purpose flour works well in this recipe and provides added nutrition.

>2 cups butter, softened
>2 cups packed brown sugar
>2 cups granulated sugar
>2 cups chunky-style peanut butter
>4 eggs
>1 tablespoon vanilla (see Homemade Vanilla, page 104)
>5 cups all-purpose flour
>1 1/2 teaspoons baking soda
>1 teaspoon baking powder
>1/2 teaspoon salt

In a large mixing bowl, cream together the butter, sugars, and peanut butter with an electric mixer. Beat in the eggs and vanilla until well combined.

In a separate large bowl, combine the flour, baking soda, baking powder, and salt. Gradually blend the dry ingredients into the creamed mixture, using a wooden spoon to stir in the last of the dry ingredients, if necessary. Combine the ingredients well.

Freeze the cookie balls according to the directions on page 105.

To bake frozen cookie balls:
Heat the oven to 350°F. Roll frozen cookie balls in granulated sugar. Place the cookies on a cookie sheet, allowing enough room for the cookies to spread while baking. Let stand about 15 minutes to partially thaw. Flatten the cookies slightly with the tines of a fork. Bake for 10 minutes or until lightly browned.

Yummy Sugar
Cookie Balls™

*M*y son, Josiah, loves it when I bake these simple sugar cookies! They're good rolled in cinnamon and sugar or frosted with Buttercream Frosting, facing page.

2 cups butter, softened
2 cups granulated sugar
2 eggs
2 teaspoons vanilla (see Homemade Vanilla, page 104)
1 teaspoon almond extract
4 cups all-purpose flour
1 teaspoon cream of tartar
1 teaspoon baking soda
1 teaspoon salt

Desserts and Breads

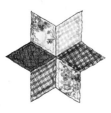

In a large mixing bowl, cream together the butter and sugar with an electric mixer. Beat in the eggs, vanilla, and almond extract until well combined.

In a separate large bowl, stir together the flour, cream of tartar, baking soda, and salt. Gradually blend the dry ingredients into the creamed mixture, using a wooden spoon to stir in the last of the dry ingredients, if necessary. Combine the ingredients well.

Freeze the cookie balls according to the directions on page 105.

To bake frozen cookie balls:
Heat the oven to 350°F. Place frozen cookie balls on a cookie sheet, allowing enough room for the cookies to spread while baking. Let stand about 10 minutes to partially thaw. Bake for 10 minutes or until lightly browned. After the cookies cool, frost them with **Freeze Ahead Buttercream Frosting,** facing page.

Freeze Ahead
Buttercream Frosting

$\mathcal{M}$ake this frosting and freeze it in small containers or self-sealing freezer storage bags. While the cookies bake, allow the frosting to thaw. At our house, when the cookies are cool enough, Josiah and Danialle have a little cookie decorating party. Remember to have lots of sprinkles on hand!

     1/3 cup butter, softened
     1 teaspoon vanilla (see Homemade Vanilla, page 104)
     2 to 3 tablespoons milk
     4 cups powdered sugar (1 pound)

In a large mixing bowl, cream together the butter and vanilla with an electric mixer. Blend in the milk. Gradually mix in the powdered sugar, 1 cup at a time, until it reaches good spreading consistency.

Divide the frosting among several small containers. Label and date the containers and freeze.

Each time you make Yummy Sugar Cookie Balls, facing page, thaw the frosting for decorating. If desired, add a small amount of food coloring to the frosting.

Easy Rolling
Pie Crust™

I used to think that making pies was such a laborious job. But now that I've learned to make this great pastry and keep it on hand in the refrigerator, it's so easy to make up a good country pie or quiche in no time at all. Try it, you'll love it! This recipe makes enough dough for four 10-inch pie crusts or five 9-inch pie crusts. Store what ever you don't use immediately in the refrigerator up to one week or in the freezer up to four months. This dough is very easy to work with, and everyone says it's the best they have ever tasted!

> 5 cups all-purpose flour
> 2 teaspoons salt
> 2 cups shortening
> 1 egg
> 1 tablespoon vinegar or lemon juice
> Water

In a large bowl, combine the flour and salt. Cut in the shortening with a pastry cutter until the pieces are the size of small peas. In a one-cup measuring cup, beat the egg. Add vinegar or lemon juice to the cup, then add enough water to equal 1 cup total. Add the egg mixture to the flour mixture, mixing until the dough forms a ball. Evenly divide the dough into 4 or 5 balls.

For immediate use, roll out dough and fit into a pie plate, following the directions on facing page.

To store unrolled dough, tightly wrap individual balls and place them in the refrigerator or freezer. Thaw in the refrigerator before using.

Denise's Tip . . . To make baking even easier for later, roll out the dough, fit it into pie plates and refrigerate or freeze until ready to use. Store in the refrigerator up to one week or in the freezer up to four months. Thaw in the refrigerator before using.

Desserts and Breads

Rolling Out Dough
For Pie Crusts

*F*or easier rolling of a stiff dough, you may warm the cold pie dough in a microwave oven for 10 to 20 seconds just before rolling it out.

Lightly flour a pastry cloth or work surface. Flatten the dough ball slightly with your hands, lightly coating the dough with flour and smoothing the edges. Use a rolling pin to roll out the dough from the center outward, shaping a circle approximately 3 inches larger in diameter than your pie plate. Without stretching the dough, gently wrap it around the rolling pin to transfer it to a pie plate. Unroll and ease the dough into the pie plate.

For a single-crust pie . . . use a knife or kitchen scissors to trim the dough about 1/2 inch beyond the rim of the pie plate. Fold under the edge of the dough even with the rim of the pie plate. Crimp the edge with your fingers or the tines of a fork. Fill or bake the pastry as directed in the recipe.

To prebake a pie shell . . . heat the oven to 450°F. Use the tines of a fork to prick the bottom and sides of the dough in several places. Bake for 8 to 12 minutes or until light golden brown; cool.

For a double-crust pie . . . trim the bottom crust slightly larger than the edge of the pie plate. Fill the pastry as directed in the recipe. Roll out the top crust. Trim the top crust to extend about 1/2 inch beyond the bottom crust and the edge of the pie plate. Moisten the perimeter edge of the bottom crust (with water, milk, or beaten egg) and fold the edge of the top crust under the bottom crust. Crimp the edges together using your fingers or the tines of a fork. Cut slits in the top crust to allow the steam to escape. Bake as directed in the recipe.

Use Easy Rolling Pie Crust™ to Make:

Danialle's Cinnamon and Sugar Pastries, page 114
Rhubarb Custard Pie, page 115
Grandma's Buttermilk 'n Berries Pie, page 116
Old Fashioned Raisin Cream Pie, page 117
Jenny's Best Pumpkin Pie, page 118
Grandma's Favorite Pecan Pie, page 119
Sue's Pig-in-Switzerland Quiche, page 10
Denise's Apple-Cheddar Quiche, page 11

Danialle's
Cinnamon and Sugar Pastries

$\mathcal{H}$ere's the perfect activity for little girls and boys who help in the kitchen. They will love rolling out leftover pie dough. Danialle enjoys serving these pastries to her brothers and they love eating them warm from the oven!

> 2 tablespoons butter, melted
> 1/4 cup sugar
> 1/4 teaspoon ground cinnamon
> Leftover dough from rolling out pie crust

Heat the oven to 350°F. Gather all the dough scraps and shape into a ball. Roll out the ball on a lightly floured surface. Cut out dough shapes with cookie cutters and place the cutouts on a cookie sheet. Brush the cutouts with melted butter. In a small bowl, combine the sugar and cinnamon and sprinkle the mixture on the dough. Bake for 5 to 10 minutes or until lightly browned. Serve warm!

Desserts and Breads

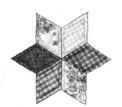

The Candy Shop

I like gumdrops, Hersheys, and Dum Dums.
All those sugary yum yums.
I go down to the store
And pick out some more
With all the money from Mum Mums.

by Josiah A. Wood, age 12
(pictured as "Bob" in "Clowns for Christ")

Rhubarb
Custard Pie

*T*his is such a wonderful pie to make in the spring when the rhubarb is up or use the frozen rhubarb available at most grocery stores. Enjoy this pie fresh from the oven or chilled, either way it's delicious.

2 Easy Rolling Pie Crusts, page 112
1 1/2 cups granulated sugar
1/4 cup all-purpose flour
1 teaspoon cornstarch
1/2 teaspoon ground nutmeg
1/2 teaspoon ground cinnamon
2 eggs, beaten
2 tablespoons butter, melted
3 to 4 cups chopped rhubarb
Milk
Granulated sugar

Heat the oven to 425°F. Roll out the dough and fit it into a 9 or 10-inch pie plate. Roll out the dough for the top crust; set aside.

In a large bowl, combine the sugar, flour, cornstarch, nutmeg, cinnamon, eggs, and butter; mix well. Stir in the rhubarb. Spread the mixture in the prepared pie plate. Cover with the top crust and crimp the edges to seal. Cut slits in the top for steam to escape. Brush the dough with milk and sprinkle with sugar. Bake at 425°F for 10 minutes. Reduce the heat to 350°F and continue baking for 40 minutes more or until nicely browned and the juices are bubbling.

To prevent the crusts from overbrowning, shape and wrap an aluminum foil collar around the edges of the pie, if needed.

When gathering rhubarb . . . grab the stalks close to the ground and pull rather than cutting the stalks at the base. Wash the stalks well, and cut them with kitchen scissors or a sharp knife.

Grandma's
Buttermilk 'n Berries Pie

Desserts
and
Breads

𝒯his refreshingly rich pie is so simple to make. Topped with fresh berries that have been tossed in Jenny's Coffee Creamers, it simply can't be beat! This pie should be chilled, so you can make it the day before serving.

> 1 cup butter, softened
> 2 cups granulated sugar
> 3 eggs, beaten
> 3 tablespoons all-purpose flour
> 1 cup buttermilk
> 1 teaspoon vanilla (see Homemade Vanilla, page 104)
> 1/4 teaspoon ground nutmeg
> 1 Easy Rolling Pie Crust, page 112
> Fresh berries for topping

Heat the oven to 350°F. Roll out the dough and fit it into a 9-inch or 10-inch pie plate.

In a large mixing bowl, cream together the butter and sugar with an electric mixer. Beat in the eggs and the flour until smooth.

In a separate bowl, blend together the buttermilk, vanilla, and nutmeg. Add to the creamed mixture and stir well to combine. Pour into the prepared pie shell. Bake for 45 to 50 minutes or until the center is firm and set. Chill for several hours or overnight.

Easy Berry Toppings

Place 2 cups sliced fresh berries in a bowl. Sprinkle the berries with 3 table-spoons of Jenny's Coffee Creamer, and toss lightly to coat the berries.

Great combinations are strawberries tossed in Jenny's French Vanilla creamer or raspberries tossed in Jenny's White Chocolate Creamer.

To serve, slice the cooled pie into 8 to 10 pieces. Top with fresh berries and a sprig of mint.

Old Fashioned
Raisin Cream Pie

$\mathcal{T}$his is an old fashioned treat that is served in many local Amish communities. The meringue adds a special touch. Try it and make it your own old fashioned tradition.

> 1 Easy Rolling Pie Crust, page 112, baked and cooled
> 1/2 cup granulated sugar
> 3 tablespoons cornstarch
> 3 eggs, separated
> 2 cups milk
> 1/2 cup raisins
> 2 teaspoons lemon juice
> 1/4 cup granulated sugar

Heat the oven to 350°F. In a small saucepan, combine the 1/2 cup sugar and the cornstarch. Stir in the egg yolks and milk. Bring to a boil over medium heat; cook and stir for 1 minute. Remove the saucepan from heat. Stir in the raisins and lemon juice, blending well. Slowly pour into the baked pie shell.

For the meringue, chill a medium size mixing bowl and beaters. In the chilled bowl, beat the egg whites with an electric mixer until foamy. Gradually add the 1/4 cup sugar while beating the egg whites. Beat until stiff peaks form (peaks stand nearly straight). Spread the meringue over the raisin filling to the edges of the pie shell. Bake for 10 to 15 minutes or until the meringue is lightly browned.

Jenny's Best
Pumpkin Pie

Most pumpkin pies just don't have enough spice for my taste. This recipe is full of spice and topped with our Pumpkin Spiced Whipped Topping, page 132, it's the perfect dessert! Don't save pumpkin pie just for the holidays—it's full of nutrition and good any time of the year. This makes two pies, one for you and one for sharing!

Desserts and Breads

2 Easy Rolling Pie Crusts, page 112
1 1/2 cups granulated sugar
1 teaspoon salt
1 tablespoon ground cinnamon
1 1/2 teaspoons ground ginger
1 teaspoon ground cloves
1/2 teaspoon ground nutmeg
4 large eggs, beaten
1 (29-ounce) can pumpkin, or 2 (15-ounce) cans pumpkin
2 (12-ounce) cans evaporated milk

Heat the oven to 425°F. Roll out the dough and fit it into two 9-inch or two 10-inch pie plates.

In a large mixing bowl, combine the sugar, salt, cinnamon, ginger, cloves, and nutmeg. Beat in the eggs and pumpkin with an electric mixer until well blended. Gradually beat in the evaporated milk.

Pour the pumpkin mixture into the prepared pie shells.

Bake at 425°F for 15 minutes, then reduce the oven temperature to 350°F. Continue baking for 40 to 50 minutes more or until the center of the pies are firm and set (a sharp knife inserted near center comes out clean).

Let the pies cool, then serve slices topped with Pumpkin Pie Whipped Topping, page 132.

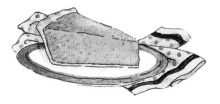

Grandma's Favorite
Pecan Pie

$\mathcal{H}$ere's an old favorite that's always a hit. Enjoy it topped with my Snickerdoodle Whipped Topping, page 132.

> 1 Easy Rolling Pie Crust, page 112
> 1 cup pecan halves
> 1/2 cup packed brown sugar
> 1 cup dark corn syrup
> 1 tablespoon butter, softened
> 1 teaspoon vanilla (see Homemade Vanilla, page 104)
> 4 eggs, slightly beaten

Heat the oven to 350°F. Roll out the dough and fit it into a 9-inch or 10-inch pie plate. Place the pecan halves in the pie shell; set aside.

In a medium mixing bowl, beat together the brown sugar, corn syrup, butter, and vanilla with an electric mixer until well combined. Beat in the eggs. Pour this mixture over the pecans in the pie shell.

Bake for 35 to 40 minutes or until the center of the pies are firm and set (a sharp knife inserted near center comes out clean), watching closely to prevent overbrowning, and cool. Slice the pie and serve topped with Snickerdoodle Whipped Topping, page 132.

Instant "Non-Stick" Measuring . . . To prevent corn syrup, honey, or any sticky ingredient from clinging to the measuring cup, first coat the cup with non-stick cooking spray before adding the ingredient. The measured amount will slip right out, ensuring you accuracy for the recipe and saving some cleanup afterward.

Crisp
Topping Mix

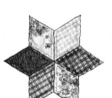

Keeping several bags of this mix on hand makes it easy to whip up a delicious and nutritious crisp any time of the year. I've included some of my favorite recipes to get you started, but you can use this mix to top just about any kind of fruit.

For two bags of mix:

4 cups old fashioned oats
1 cup all-purpose flour
2 cups packed brown sugar
1 teaspoon ground cinnamon

In a large bowl, combine all the ingredients and stir to mix well. Label and date two self-sealing storage bags. Evenly divide the mix (approximately 3 1/2 cups each) between the two bags and seal them tightly.

To Make Crisp Topping:

1 bag Crisp Topping Mix
1 stick (1/2 cup) butter, softened

In a medium bowl, cut the butter into the mix until well combined. Sprinkle the topping mix over your favorite crisp recipe.

Use Crisp Topping Mix for These Recipes:

• Denise's Perfectly Peach Crisp, page 121
• Triple Berry Crisp, page 122
• Josh's Strawberry-Rhubarb Crisp, page 123
• So Simple Spiced Apple Crisp, page 124

Most crisp recipes . . . that call for a 9x13-inch baking pan can easily be made into two 8-inch square baking pans. Bake one of the crisps now and freeze one to bake later. When baking a frozen crisp, reduce the oven temperature to 325°F and extend the baking time to slightly longer than needed for an unfrozen crisp. Watch closely to prevent overbrowning and bake just until the topping is lightly browned and the filling is bubbly.

Desserts and Breads

Denise's
Perfectly Peach Crisp

What could be easier than making peach crisp with canned peaches and a bag of Crisp Topping Mix? Denise's special spices really add a nice touch!

2 (29-ounce) cans sliced peaches in heavy syrup
1/2 teaspoon ground ginger
1 teaspoon ground cinnamon
1 teaspoon ground nutmeg
1/4 cup all-purpose flour
2 teaspoons vanilla (see Homemade Vanilla, page 104)
1 bag Crisp Topping Mix, facing page
1 stick (1/2 cup) butter, softened

Heat the oven to 350°F. Drain the peaches, reserving 1 cup of the syrup. Place the peaches in one 9x13-inch baking dish or two 8-inch square baking pans.

In a small bowl, combine the reserved syrup, ginger, cinnamon, nutmeg, vanilla, and flour and mix well. Pour the syrup mixture over the peaches.

In a separate bowl, cut the butter into the Crisp Topping Mix until well combined. Sprinkle over the peaches. Bake for 1 hour or until the topping is lightly browned and the filling is bubbly.

White Chocolate Whipped Topping

1/2 cup whipping cream
3 tablespoons Jenny's Winter White Chocolate Dessert Coffee Creamer

Chill a glass mixing bowl and beaters in the refrigerator. Combine the whipping cream and coffee creamer in the bowl and stir together to dissolve the creamer. Beat on high speed with an electric mixer until stiff peaks form. Use to top hot drinks or desserts.

Serve warm with a dollop of White Chocolate Whipped Topping, recipe above.

Triple
Berry Crisp

My dad enjoys this crisp served hot in a bowl with a little cream over the top! Almost any mix of berries would work, but I like the ease of using the pre-mixed triple berry blend available at most grocery stores.

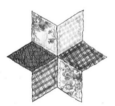

Desserts and Breads

2 (1-pound) packages frozen triple berry blend
    (or equivalent fresh or frozen berries)
1 1/4 cups granulated sugar
1/4 cup all-purpose flour
1 bag Crisp Topping Mix, page 120
1 stick butter, softened (1/2 cup)

Heat the oven to 350°F. Lightly oil a 9x13-inch baking dish or a 2-quart baking dish for a deeper crisp.

In a large bowl, combine the berries, sugar, and flour; mix together well. Spoon the berry mixture into the prepared baking dish.

In a separate bowl, cut the butter into the Crisp Topping Mix until well combined. Sprinkle over the berries. Bake for 45 minutes or until the topping is lightly browned and the filling is bubbly.

Serve with Jenny's French Vanilla Creamer and Jenny's Cafe Blend Coffee!

Josh's
Strawberry-Rhubarb Crisp

*J*osh came up with this idea one day when I was going to make a Rhubarb Crisp—and it was a hit! It's so easy to make with frozen sliced and sweetened strawberries.

4 to 5 cups chopped rhubarb
2 (16-ounce) packages frozen sweetened and sliced strawberries, thawed
1/4 cup quick-cooking tapioca
1 bag Crisp Topping Mix, page 120
1 stick butter, softened (1/2 cup)

Heat the oven to 350°F. Lightly oil a 9x13-inch baking dish or two 8-inch square baking dishes.

In a bowl, combine the rhubarb, strawberries, and tapioca. Spread the fruit mixture in the prepared baking dish or dishes.

In a separate bowl, cut the butter into the Crisp Topping Mix until well combined. Sprinkle the mixture over the fruit. Bake for 45 minutes or until the topping is lightly browned and the filling is bubbly.

Serve warm with a big scoop of vanilla ice cream.

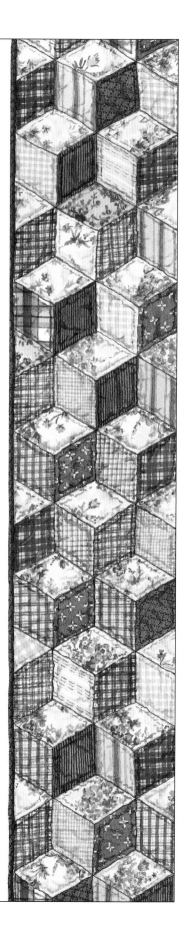

So Simple
Spiced Apple Crisp

*I*t's easy to whip up this recipe using Jenny's Mulling Spices and a bag of Crisp Topping Mix, page 120.

1 package Jenny's Mulling Spices
2 tablespoons all-purpose flour
7 cups peeled, cored, and sliced apples
1 bag Crisp Topping Mix, page 120
1 stick butter, softened (1/2 cup)

Heat the oven to 350°F. Lightly oil one 9x13 or two 8-inch square baking dishes.

In a large bowl, mix together the mulling spices and flour. Toss in the apples, stirring to coat with the spice mixture. Evenly spread the coated apples in the prepared baking dish or dishes.

In a separate bowl, cut the butter into the Crisp Topping Mix until well combined. Sprinkle the mixture over the apples. Bake for 45 minutes or until the topping is lightly browned and the filling is bubbly.

Serve warm with vanilla ice cream and a drizzling of Amish Caramel Sauce, page 132.

Turtle Fudge
Pudding Cake

*T*his recipe was requested by my good friend Melinda, who has helped us through the busy holiday season nearly every year since the beginning of Jenny's Country Kitchen. A special thanks to her and to Sheri for all their hard work.

2 tablespoons butter, softened
1 cup granulated sugar
1 teaspoon vanilla (see Homemade Vanilla, page 104)
1 cup all-purpose flour
4 tablespoons cocoa powder, divided
1 teaspoon baking powder
1/2 teaspoon salt
3/4 cup milk
1/2 cup chopped pecans
1/2 cup packed dark brown sugar
1 tablespoon butter
1 tablespoon cornstarch
1 2/3 cups boiling water

Heat the oven to 350°F. Grease an 8-inch square baking pan.

In a large mixing bowl, cream together the butter, sugar, and vanilla with an electric mixer.

In a medium bowl, combine the flour, 3 tablespoons of the cocoa powder, the baking powder, and salt. Add the dry ingredients to the creamed mixture and mix well. Add the milk and mix well again. Stir in the nuts. Spread the batter in the prepared baking pan.

In a separate bowl, mix together the brown sugar, the remaining 1 tablespoon cocoa powder, butter, corn starch, and the boiling water. Gently pour this mixture over the cake batter in the baking pan. Bake for 40 minutes or until done.

This cake makes it's own sauce at the bottom and is delicious served warm with a big scoop of vanilla ice cream.

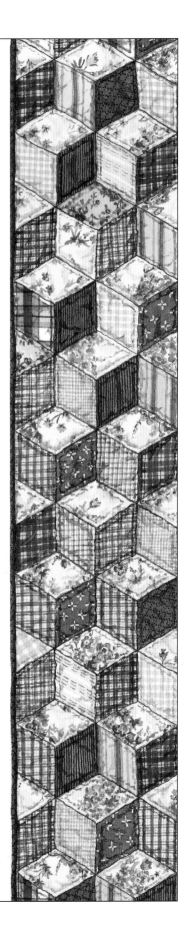

Carrot
Cake Mix

*T*his is one of my signature baking mixes that started Jenny's Country Kitchen®. Each bag of mix is enough for one 9x13-inch or two 8-inch square cakes. Freeze slices of the baked and frosted cake to pack in cold lunches or for easy after-school snacks.

Desserts and Breads

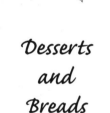

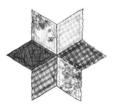

For 2 bags of mix:

4 cups all-purpose flour
4 cups granulated sugar
2 teaspoons baking soda
2 teaspoons salt
4 teaspoons ground cinnamon

In a very large bowl, combine all the ingredients and stir until well mixed. Label and date two large self-sealing storage bags. Evenly divide the mix between the two bags (approximately 4 cups each). Seal the bags.

To make Carrot Cake:

4 eggs
1 1/2 cups vegetable oil
1 bag Carrot Cake Mix
3 cups grated carrots
1/2 cup raisins, optional
1/2 cup chopped walnuts, optional

Heat the oven to 350°F. Generously oil one 9x13-inch or two 8-inch square baking pans; set aside.

In a large mixing bowl, beat together the eggs and oil with an electric mixer. Add the Carrot Cake Mix and beat well. Fold in the carrots, raisins, and walnuts. Pour into the prepared baking pan or pans. Bake for 50 minutes or until a knife inserted in the center comes out clean. Let the cake cool.

Frost the cooled cake with Cream Cheese Frosting, facing page.

Serve with Jenny's French Vanilla Creamer and Jenny's Cafe Blend Coffee!

Canned
Carrot Cake

$\mathcal{H}$ere's a unique way to bake and store carrot cake to give as gifts or to enjoy by the fireplace with a cup of Jenny's Cinnamon Cocoa.

Heat the oven to 350°F. Oil five wide mouth 1-pint canning jars; set aside.

Make the carrot cake batter as instructed on facing page. Pour approximately 1 cup plus 1 tablespoon of batter into each jar, filling them slightly more than half full and less than two-thirds full. Wipe the rims of the jars clean. Bake the jars of batter for approximately 50 minutes or until a knife inserted in the center comes out clean.

While the cakes are baking, place five wide mouth lids and rings in a small saucepan. Cover them with water, bring the water to a boil, and boil for 5 minutes. When the cakes are done, immediately place one lid and ring on each jar, sealing tightly. As the cakes cool, the lids seal. When completely cooled, store the cakes in a cool dark place until ready to eat.

Frost with Cream Cheese Frosting, recipe below. Divide the frosting among small self-sealing storage bags and freeze until ready to use. Thaw the frosting and spread it on the cake before serving.

Cream Cheese Frosting

1 (8-ounce) package cream cheese, softened
2 tablespoons butter, softened
1 teaspoon vanilla (see Homemade Vanilla, page 104)
2 to 3 tablespoons milk
1 pound (4 cups) powdered sugar

In a large mixing bowl, cream together the cream cheese, butter, and vanilla with an electric mixer. Blend in the milk. Gradually mix in the powdered sugar, 1 cup at a time, until desired spreading consistency. Spread the frosting on cooled Carrot Cake, Farmer's Market Pumpkin Bars, page 128, or any other cake.

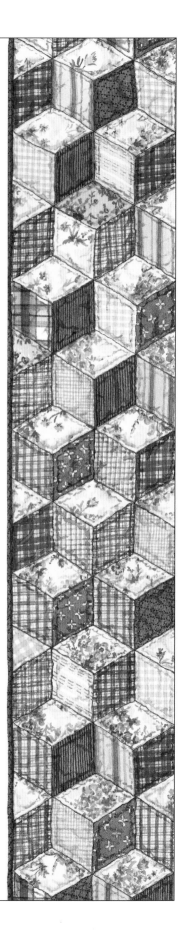

Farmer's Market
Pumpkin Bars

*U*se canned pumpkin, freshly cooked pumpkin, or any squash variety in this recipe. I bake these bars to make good use of my dad's abundant squash crop, and over the years I have sold many of these bars at the local farmer's market.

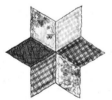

4 eggs
2 cups granulated sugar
1 cup vegetable oil
1 (15-ounce) can pumpkin or 2 cups cooked squash or pumpkin
2 cups flour (I combine 1 1/2 cups all-purpose and 1/2 cup whole wheat)
2 teaspoons baking powder
1 teaspoon baking soda
3/4 teaspoon salt
2 teaspoons ground cinnamon
Cream Cheese Frosting, page 127
Candy sprinkles for topping

Heat the oven to 350°F. Lightly grease and flour a 15x10-inch jelly-roll pan; set aside.

In a large mixing bowl, beat the eggs with an electric mixer until foamy. Add the sugar, oil, and pumpkin; continue to beat at medium speed about 2 minutes, combining well.

In a medium bowl, combine the flour, baking powder, baking soda, salt, and cinnamon. Add the dry ingredients to the pumpkin mixture; beat on low speed for 1 minute. Pour the batter into the prepared pan. Bake for 25 to 30 minutes or until a toothpick inserted in the center comes out clean. Cool, frost, and decorate.

To add a special touch, make the cream cheese frosting and mix in 2-3 tablespoons of Jenny's Pumpkin Pie Coffee Creamer. Mix well and spread on cooled bars. Top with sprinkles.

Cooking Pumpkin or Squash . . . Heat oven to 350°F. Wash and cut each unpeeled squash or pumpkin in half or quarter sections. Remove seeds and place cut side down in a 9x13-inch baking pan. Add about one inch of water to the pan. Cover with foil and bake for about 30 to 50 minutes or until tender. Cool slightly and scrape from skins. Use in recipes now or freeze for later.

Double Chocolate
Layer Bars

I can still remember visiting my Grandma Merkel's house in Spring Valley, Minnesota, where these were often waiting on the table! My special touch is using two kinds of chocolate chips. These are quick as a wink and oh, so good!

1/2 cup butter
1 1/2 cups graham cracker crumbs
   (or 12 graham cracker rectangles, crushed)
1 cup chopped pecans or walnuts
3/4 cup semi-sweet chocolate chips
3/4 cup white chocolate chips
1 1/2 cups flaked coconut
1 (14-ounce) can sweetened condensed milk

Heat the oven to 350°F. Place the butter in a 9 x13-inch baking pan and place the pan in the oven to melt the butter. Remove the pan from the oven and mix in the graham cracker crumbs. Spread the crumbs in the pan, using the back of a spoon to press crumbs evenly. Sprinkle on the nuts, then the chips, then the coconut.

Drizzle the sweetened condensed milk over all.

Bake for 25 minutes or until lightly browned. Cool completely before cutting into bars (unless you're like me and must sneak one while they're still warm!)

For graham cracker crumbs . . . place the crackers in a large self-sealing storage bag and use a rolling pin to crush them.

Pantry-Stocking
Brownie Mix

*T*his recipe makes a big container of mix that makes 8 batches of brownies. They're easy to bake when you're having a chocolate attack and the mix looks beautiful in an antique 2-quart jar. My friends often request it as a gift.

> 4 cups all-purpose flour
> 6 cups granulated sugar
> 3 cups unsweetened cocoa powder
> 4 teaspoons baking powder
> 3 teaspoons salt
> 2 cups butter-flavored shortening*

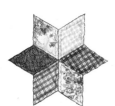

Desserts and Breads

In a large bowl, mix together all the dry ingredients. Using a pastry blender, cut in the shortening until thoroughly mixed. Store in an airtight container in a cool dry place. *Sometimes I use real butter in place of the shortening and then keep it stored in the refrigerator.

To make brownies with the mix:

> 2 cups Brownie Mix
> 2 eggs, beaten
> 1 teaspoon vanilla (see Homemade Vanilla, page 104)
> 1/2 cup chopped walnuts, optional

Heat the oven to 350°F. Lightly grease or oil an 8-inch square baking pan.

In a large bowl, stir together all the ingredients until well mixed. Spread the batter in the prepared pan. Bake for 20 to 25 minutes or until set in the center.

Check out the Double Chocolate Brownie Sundae recipe, facing page.

Phil's
Chocolate Syrup

*P*hil is Denise's husband; Denise is our wonderful test cook here at Jenny's Country Kitchen. This syrup is perfect over vanilla ice cream, to make chocolate milk, or on our Double Chocolate Brownie Sundae. It will keep up to 3 weeks in the fridge—if it lasts that long!

> 3 cups granulated sugar
> 2 cups water
> 1 cup unsweetened cocoa powder
> 2 teaspoons vanilla (see Homemade Vanilla, page 104)

In a saucepan, mix together the sugar, water, and cocoa powder. Bring to a boil over medium heat; boil for 3 minutes, stirring constantly. Remove from heat and stir in the vanilla. Allow the syrup to cool. This syrup can be warmed in the microwave on medium for 20-30 seconds.

Double Chocolate Brownie Sundae

Here's where you can bring several delicious recipes into one super-dooper all-out splurging treat!

> 1 warm Brownie, facing page
> 1 large scoop vanilla ice cream
> Phil's Chocolate Syrup, warmed, recipe above
> Jenny's White Chocolate Whipped Topping, page 132
> Chopped pecans
> Maraschino cherries

Assemble in the order listed and enjoy with a cup of Jenny's Café Blend Coffee.

Amish
Caramel Sauce

Desserts and Breads

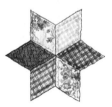

*T*his delicious caramel sauce is very easy to make and it freezes well. If you just can't manage to eat it all, freeze portions of it in small self-sealing containers. Drizzle the sauce over So Simple Spiced Apple Crisp, page 124, or use it to top ice cream.

> 3 sticks butter (1 1/2 cups)
> 3 cups brown sugar
> 1 1/2 teaspoons salt
> 1 (12-ounce) can evaporated milk
> 1 tablespoon vanilla (see Homemade Vanilla, page 104)

Melt the butter in a saucepan over medium heat. Stir in the brown sugar and salt; bring to a boil, stirring constantly with a wire whisk. Gradually add the evaporated milk. Return the mixture to boiling, stirring constantly, and continue boilng for 5 minutes longer.

Remove from heat and stir in the vanilla. The sauce will be slightly thinner than caramel sauce purchased from the store, but twice as flavorful! Serve warm or cooled. This sauce can be warmed in the microwave on medium for 20-30 seconds.

Jenny's
Easy Whipped Topping

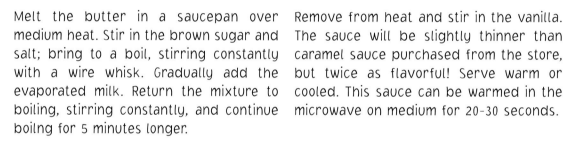

It's so easy to make flavored whipped topping by combining whipping cream with any of Jenny's Dessert Coffee Creamers.

> 1/2 cup whipping cream
> 3 tablespoons Jenny's Dessert Coffee Creamer, any flavor

Chill a glass mixing bowl and beaters in the refrigerator. Combine the whipping cream and coffee creamer in the bowl and stir together to dissolve the creamer. Beat on high speed with an electric mixer until stiff peaks form. Use to top pies, cakes, cocoa, or anything your heart desires!

Try Pumpkin Pie, Snickerdoodle, Winter White Chocolate and French Vanilla.

Farmer's Market
Banana Bread

*I*t is just as easy to make four loaves of banana bread as it is to make two if you have enough bananas—and quick breads also freeze well. You can eat one or two, then freeze the extras to pull out and serve when you have drop-in guests. If you can't possibly find any more room in your freezer, then this will be a wonderful opportunity for you to be neighborly!

For 2 loaves:	Ingredient	For 4 loaves:
2 cups	granulated sugar	4 cups
3 to 4	medium size bananas	6 to 8
3/4 cup	butter, softened	1 1/2 cups
1/4 cup	olive oil*	1/2 cup
1/2 cup	milk	1 cup
1 tablespoon	vanilla (page 104)	2 tablespoons
4	eggs	8
3 1/4 cups	all-purpose flour	6 1/2 cups
3/4 cup	whole wheat flour	1 1/2 cups
2 teaspoons	baking soda	4 teaspoons
1 teaspoon	salt	2 teaspoons
3/4 cup	chopped walnuts, optional	1 1/2 cups

Heat the oven to 350°F. Grease and set aside the loaf pans.

In a large mixing bowl, combine the sugar, bananas, butter, oil, milk, vanilla, and eggs. Mix for 1 to 2 minutes at medium speed with an electric mixer.

In a separate large bowl, lightly stir together the flours, baking soda, and salt. Add the dry ingredients to the banana mixture and stir just until moistened. Fold in the nuts, if desired. Evenly spread the batter into the prepared loaf pans. Bake about 50 minutes or until a knife inserted in the center comes out clean. Cool slightly before removing from the pans and enjoy with a pat of real butter!

*Butter can be substituted for the olive oil.

To freeze the loaves . . . allow them to cool, and then wrap in a double thickness of aluminum foil. Freeze up to 6 months.

Grandma Trudy's
Zucchini Bread

*W*hen Dan and I married, Dan's mother, Trudy, gave us a little book of her favorite recipes. It included this one, which is one of my favorites! This recipe makes two full-size loaves or four small loaves for gift giving, or selling at the local farmer's market—like I did.

3 eggs
1 cup vegetable oil
2 cups granulated sugar
2 cups grated zucchini (I usually leave the peels on and the seeds in.)
3 tablespoons vanilla (see Homemade Vanilla, page 104)
3 cups flour (I combine 2 cups all-purpose and 1 cup whole wheat)
1 teaspoon salt
1 1/2 teaspoons baking powder
1 teaspoon baking soda
4 teaspoons ground cinnamon
1 cup chopped walnuts, optional

Heat the oven to 350°F. Grease and flour 2 large or 4 mini loaf pans*.

In a large mixing bowl, beat the eggs until light and foamy. Beat in the oil, sugar, zucchini, and vanilla until well blended.

In a separate bowl, combine the flour, salt, baking powder, baking soda, and cinnamon. Add the dry ingredients to the zucchini mixture and stir just until dry ingredients are moistened. Fold in the nuts, if desired. Evenly spread the batter into the prepared loaf pans.

Bake about 1 hour or until a toothpick inserted in the center comes out clean. Cool slightly before removing from the baking pans.

Mini loaf pans . . . make a cute gift to share with a friend or neighbor. Wrap them in decorative or colored plastic wrap and tie with a ribbon. *When baking mini loaves, remember to reduce the cooking time. Check after 30 minutes, when done, a toothpick inserted in the center will come out clean.

Desserts and Breads

Joel's Freezer
Cheddar Biscuits

*T*hese biscuits are scrumptious and easy to make. You can freeze the shaped dough and take out the amount you need for each meal.

> 2 1/4 cups all-purpose flour
> 1 tablespoon baking powder
> 1/2 teaspoon garlic powder
> 1/4 teaspoon onion salt
> 1/4 teaspoon salt
> 1 1/4 cups butter, softened
> 1 1/2 cups shredded cheddar cheese
> 1 1/4 cups milk

In a large mixing bowl, combine the flour, baking powder, garlic powder, onion salt and salt. Cut in the softened butter with a pastry blender until small pea-size pieces form. Mix in the cheese and milk to form a soft ball.

Drop by rounded spoonfuls onto baking sheets; freeze for 1 hour. Transfer the biscuits to a tightly sealing storage container. The frozen biscuits stay fresh up to 6 months.

To bake frozen biscuits:
Heat the oven to 450°F. Place frozen biscuits on a baking sheet. Bake about 15 minutes or until golden brown and flaky.

Freezer-Stocking
Baking Powder Biscuits

*B*ecause this recipe makes a large batch, you can bake some now and freeze the remaining dough for later.

4 1/2 cups all-purpose flour
2 tablespoons baking powder
2 1/2 teaspoons salt
2 tablespoons sugar
2 sticks butter (1 cup), softened, not melted
2 cups milk

Heat the oven to 425°F. In a large bowl, combine the flour, baking powder, salt, and sugar. Cut in the butter with a pastry blender until small pea-size pieces form. Mix in the milk to form a soft ball.

On a lightly floured surface, knead the dough for 1 minute. Pat the dough into a circle about 3/4 inch thick. Cut the dough with a large biscuit cutter. Place the biscuits 1-inch apart on a baking sheet. Bake about 15 minutes, or until golden brown.

To freeze the remaining unbaked biscuits, place them on a baking sheet and freeze for 1 hour. Transfer to a tightly sealing storage container. Label and date the container, and freeze the biscuits up to 6 months.

To bake the frozen biscuits:
Heat the oven to 400°F. Place the biscuits 1-inch apart on a baking sheet. Bake about 20 minutes or until golden brown.

Serve these warm out of the oven with butter and Fresh 'n Simple Strawberry Jam, page 31.

Desserts and Breads

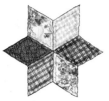

Applesauce and Raisin Bran
Refrigerator Muffins

*Y*ou'll love this muffin recipe, even my children love them! They're the perfect way to start your day, along with a glass of juice or a cup of Jenny's House Blend Coffee. Store the batter in the refrigerator up to two weeks, although it never lasts that long at my house.

1 (15-ounce) box Raisin Bran cereal
3 cups granulated sugar
5 cups all-purpose flour
1 tablespoon + 2 teaspoons baking soda
2 teaspoons salt
1 1/2 teaspoons ground nutmeg
1 tablespoon ground cinnamon
2 cups applesauce
1 cup shortening
4 eggs, beaten
1 quart buttermilk

In a very large bowl, mix together the cereal, sugar, flour, baking soda, salt, nutmeg, and cinnamon.

In a separate mixing bowl, beat together the applesauce, shortening, and eggs until well combined. Beat in the buttermilk. Add the applesauce mixture to the dry ingredients and mix well.

To bake some of the muffins now, heat the oven to 400°F. Grease or line muffin cups. Fill the cups two-thirds full with batter. Bake for 15 minutes or until golden brown and a toothpick inserted near the center of a muffin comes out clean. Tightly cover the remaining batter and store it in the refrigerator up to two weeks.

To bake the refrigerated batter . . . increase the baking time slightly, to approximately 20 minutes. Muffins will be done when golden brown and a toothpick inserted near the center of a muffin comes out clean.

Carrot-Raisin
Muffins

*T*his delicious muffin is chock full of nutrition. What's great about this recipe is that it can be easily doubled and the batter can be frozen for up to six months. See instructions on facing page.

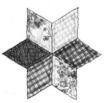

Desserts and Breads

2 cups whole-wheat flour
2 teaspoons baking soda
2 teaspoons ground cinnamon
1/2 teaspoon salt
2 eggs
1 cup honey
1 (8-ounce) carton plain yogurt
1/4 cup applesauce
1/4 cup light olive oil or vegetable oil
2 teaspoons lemon juice
2 teaspoons vanilla (see Homemade Vanilla, page 104)
1 1/2 cups shredded carrots
1 cup raisins
1/2 cup chopped walnuts, optional

Heat the oven to 350°F. Grease or line 12 muffin cups; set aside.

In a large mixing bowl, combine the flour, soda, cinnamon, and salt.

In a separate bowl, mix together the eggs, honey, yogurt, applesauce, oil, lemon juice, and vanilla. Stir the egg mixture into the dry ingredients just until blended. Fold in the carrots, raisins, and nuts, if desired.

Fill the muffin cups two-thirds full. Bake for 20 to 25 minutes or until a toothpick inserted near the center of a muffin comes out clean.

Sweet Potato
Muffins

These dense muffins taste so very good. Here's another recipe that can easily be doubled and the batter frozen for up to six months. Using Raw Turbinado sugar for topping muffins looks extra pretty and can be found in most grocery stores.

1/2 cup butter
1 1/4 cups granulated sugar
2 eggs
1/3 cup milk
1 1/4 cups mashed sweet potatoes, squash, or pumpkin
1 1/2 cups whole wheat flour
2 teaspoons baking powder
1/4 teaspoon salt
2 teaspoons ground cinnamon
1/2 teaspoon ground nutmeg
Raw turbinado sugar for topping

Heat the oven to 400°F. Grease or line 12 muffin cups; set aside.

In a large mixing bowl, cream together the butter and sugar with an electric mixer. Add the eggs, milk, and mashed sweet potatoes and continue creaming.

In a separate bowl, stir together the flour, baking powder, salt, cinnamon, and nutmeg. Add the dry ingredients to the creamed mixture, stirring just until moistened.

Fill the muffin cups two-thirds full and sprinkle the muffin tops with raw turbinado sugar. Bake about 20 minutes or until a toothpick inserted in the center of a muffin comes out clean.

Freezing Muffin Batter . . . You can easily double any muffin recipe and freeze the leftover batter in heavy-duty gallon size freezer bags. Label and date the bags, then freeze the batter up to six months. To use the batter, simply thaw the mix in the bag, snip off one bottom corner of the bag, and squeeze the batter into muffin cups. Bake as directed. Voila, instant satisfaction!

Fresh Berry
Muffin Mix

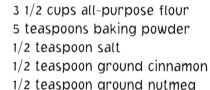

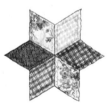

Another great way to make muffin-making a little easier is to have some mixes stocked in your pantry. This recipe makes two batches. When preparing the batter, mix in any fresh berries of the season for a delicious and easy-to-make muffin.

> 3 1/2 cups all-purpose flour
> 5 teaspoons baking powder
> 1/2 teaspoon salt
> 1/2 teaspoon ground cinnamon
> 1/2 teaspoon ground nutmeg
> 1 cup granulated sugar
> 1/3 cup nonfat dry milk

In a large bowl, mix together all ingredients. Label and date two self-sealing storage bags. Evenly divide the mix (approximately 2 1/2 cups each) between the two bags and seal to store.

To make muffins using the mix:

> 1 egg, well beaten
> 1/3 cup vegetable oil or
>   melted butter
> 2/3 cup water
> 1 bag Berry Muffin Mix
> 1 cup fresh raspberries,
>   blueberries, or black berries
> Granulated sugar

Heat the oven to 400°F. Grease or line 12 muffin cups; set aside.

In a large bowl, mix together the egg, oil or butter, and water. Stir in the dry Berry Muffin Mix, stirring just until the dry ingredients are moistened. Fold in the berries.

Fill the muffin cups two-thirds full and sprinkle the muffin tops with sugar. Bake 20 to 25 minutes or until a toothpick inserted in the center of a muffin comes out clean.

When mixing muffin batter . . . gently mix the dry ingredients into the creamed mixture until just moist. Overmixing causes the muffins to peak and have air bubbles.

Country
Corn Bread and Muffin Mix

*H*ere's a great mix to stock in your pantry! Use it to bake up some corn muffins or bread, Chilean Eggs, page 14, or to top Easy Tamale Pie, page 45.

> 2 cups all-purpose flour
> 1 1/2 cups yellow cornmeal
> 3 tablespoons baking powder
> 1/2 cup granulated sugar
> 1 1/2 teaspoons salt

In a large bowl, mix together all ingredients. Label and date two self-sealing storage bags. Evenly divide the mix (approximately 2 1/4 cups each) between the two bags and seal to store.

To make muffins from the mix:

> 1 egg, well beaten
> 1/4 cup butter, melted
> 1 cup milk
> 1 bag Country Corn Bread & Muffin Mix

Heat the oven to 400°F. Grease or line 12 muffin cups; set aside.

In a small bowl, combine the egg, butter, and milk; stir just until blended. Stir in the corn bread and muffin mix just until the dry ingredients are moistened (do not overmix).

Fill muffin cups two-thirds full. Bake for 20 minutes or until muffin tops are golden brown and firm to the touch.

To make corn bread, or johnny cake . . . Spread the batter in a greased 8-inch square baking pan. Bake 20 minutes or until the top is golden brown and firm to the touch.

Quick Substitutions and Equivalents

1 package active dry yeast = 1 tablespoon dry or 1 cake compressed yeast
1 teaspoon baking powder = 1/2 teaspoon cream of tartar plus 1/4 teaspoon baking soda
1 cup whole milk = 1 cup skim or reconstituted nonfat dry milk plus 2 teaspoons butter
1 pound granulated sugar = 2 cups granulated sugar

1 pound brown sugar = 2 1/4 cups firmly packed brown sugar

1 pound powdered sugar = 4 cups unsifted powdered sugar

1 cup granulated sugar = 1 cup firmly packed brown sugar or 2 cups sifted powdered sugar

1 cup buttermilk = 1 tablespoon vinegar or lemon juice plus milk to equal 1 cup. Let stand for 5 minutes.
  Or use 1 cup plain yogurt.

1 tablespoon cornstarch = 2 tablespoons flour (for thickening); or for fruit desserts, 1 1/3 tablespoons
  quick-cooking tapioca.

1/2 cup corn syrup = 1/2 cup sugar plus 2 tablespoons water

1 teaspoon dried mustard (in cooked mixtures) = 1 tablespoon prepared mustard

1 tablespoon fresh herbs = 1 teaspoon dried herbs, or 1/8 teaspoon powdered herbs

1 garlic clove = 1/8 teaspoon garlic powder or 1/2 teaspoon garlic salt

1 cup half and half = 7/8 cup milk plus 3 tablespoons butter

1 cup heavy whipping cream (for baking, not whipping) = 3/4 cup whole milk plus 1/4 cup butter

1 small onion, chopped = 1 teaspoon onion powder or 1 tablespoon dried minced onion

1 (8-ounce) carton sour cream = 1 cup sour cream

1 cup tomato juice = 1/2 cup tomato sauce plus 1/2 cup water

1 bouillon cube = 1 teaspoon instant bouillon

Weights and Measurements

1 tablespoon = 3 teaspoons
1/8 cup = 2 tablespoons or 1 fluid ounce
1/4 cup = 4 tablespoons or 2 fluid ounces
1/3 cup = 5 1/3 tablespoons
1/2 cup = 8 tablespoons or 4 fluid ounces
2/3 cup = 10 2/3 tablespoons
3/4 cup = 12 tablespoons
1 cup = 16 tablespoons or 8 fluid ounces
2 cups = 1 pint or 16 fluid ounces
2 pints = 1 quart or 32 fluid ounces
4 quarts = 1 gallon
4 ounces of cheese = 1 cup shredded
8 ounces of cheese = 2 cups shredded
1 pound of cheese = 4 cups shredded

Index

Red = base recipes used in many recipes
Blue = pantry-stocking mixes
Green = freezer-stocking recipes
Purple = slow-cooked recipes